Contents

KU-422-562

THE TECHNOLOGY

THE EQUIPMENT

THE PRODUCTION PROCESS

N

STANDARD LOAN

UNLESS RECALLED BY ANOTHER READER
THIS ITEM MAY BE BORROWED FOR

FOUR WEEKS

To renew, online at: http://pri.
or by telephone: 01243 81⁶'
012⁴ˑ

;-Camera Video
ɔduction

m

MEDIA MANUALS

Single-Camera Video Production

Robert B. Musburger

FOCAL PRESS
Boston   London

To my mother, Mary Tomazina Wemple Musburger Houska, for teaching me the value of integrating art and technology.

Focal Press is an imprint of Butterworth–Heinemann.

Library of Congress Cataloging-in-Publication Data
Musburger, Robert B.
    Single-camera video production / Robert Musburger.
      p.   cm. — (Media manuals)
    Includes bibliographical references and index.
    ISBN 0-240-80034-6 (pbk. : alk. paper)
    1. Video tape recorders and recording. 2. Video recordings—
Production and direction. I. Title. II. Series.
TK6655.V5M88   1993   92-13909
778.5'99—dc20

British Library Cataloguing-in-Publication Data
A catalogue record for this book is available from the British Library.

Butterworth–Heinemann
313 Washington Street
Newton, MA 02158–1626

10 9 8 7 6 5 4

Printed in the United States of America

POSTPRODUCTION

Introduction

This text has been written to provide three groups of video enthusiasts with enough information to produce acceptable single-camera video productions: the media production student, the professional who needs a refresher in the basics, and the first-time video camera owner. It is a basic, introductory book designed to point the beginner in the right direction.

This is not an advanced book in preproduction research and writing, nor is it a book on advanced techniques in electronic editing. Each of those subjects deserves its own title.

I wrote this book from three points of view: first, from that of an instructor introducing the techniques that lead to quality video productions utilizing a single video camera; second, from that of a practitioner who has spent 40 years working in professional television and learning the contents of this book the hard way—by making mistakes until I finally got it right; and third, from that of an academic fielding 20 phone calls a week from people new to electronic production who desperately want information in single-camera video production.

I will outline the process of working with a single video camera from beginning to end, with an emphasis on the actual production process. First, though, you must lay some groundwork before you pick up your camera. The video camera and recorder remain two complex pieces of equipment, despite efforts to simplify them. The process by which a video image is created is also complex and you must understand it in order to properly utilize the benefits and master the restrictions of the medium.

The first section contains a simplified explanation of how and why the video and audio signals are created and of the technical restrictions that exist within a video system. The second section contains descriptions of the equipment: cameras; recorders; and audio, lighting, and mounting equipment. With the first two sections providing a firm base, the third section carries you through the production process from preproduction planning (much more important than most beginners realize) to setting up, rehearsing, shooting, and striking. The final section touches on the postproduction process and the importance of shooting for the editing process.

Acknowledgments

One cannot work in the video business without relying on many other people. This is not a solitary business, and throughout the years many people have made major contributions to my knowledge and career. Without creating a boring litany, here are a few of many: Parks Whitmer and Sam Scott, who started me in media production and kept me going; Art Mosby, who paid my first television paycheck; Bob Wormington, who let me develop my directing skills; the thousands of students at Avila, UMKC, KU, FSU, and UH who constantly reminded me I don't know everything there is to know about media production, and my wife, Pat, who lets me think I do.

Credit for the illustrations for this book is shared by three of my students: Sean Berry, Jan Lockett, and Jeff Lyon. Someday may we all work in the same computer format.

And especially all of the helpful people at Focal Press who have guided and prodded me through my first publishing efforts: Karen, Philip, Mary, Trish, and Maggie.

The Importance of Technology

If a would-be artist were to suddenly pick up a brush and start to dab paint on a canvas, or any other handy surface, the chances of achieving an immediate masterpiece would be minimal. The same holds true of a sculptor. One does not attack a piece of marble with a chisel without first learning the skills necessary to properly mold the form without damaging the original material or exceeding the capabilities of the medium.

Likewise, running through the woods with an out-of-focus camera may seem creative, but it is neither good art nor good video. An understanding of the basic technology of any art form is necessary in order to properly utilize the artistic characteristics of that medium and to avoid the pitfalls of its technical limitations.

Video is highly technical; the medium requires some basic knowledge of optics, electronics, electricity, physics, and mathematics. Of course, a video production can be completed without any knowledge of the subjects just listed, but the possibility of it being a top-quality production is very limited.

In order to utilize the video camera and associated audio equipment effectively, you must be aware of the capabilities as well as the limitations of each piece of equipment. In addition, you must know how each piece of equipment operates in relation to other equipment used in the same production. This awareness does not necessarily mean having a broad range of knowledge of the sciences involved in media production, but rather an appreciation and understanding of why the equipment is designed to operate as it does and what it can accomplish. Most important, it is necessary to understand what it *cannot* be expected to accomplish.

PLANNED ART
VS. UNPLANNED ART

Art by Accident

Art by Plan

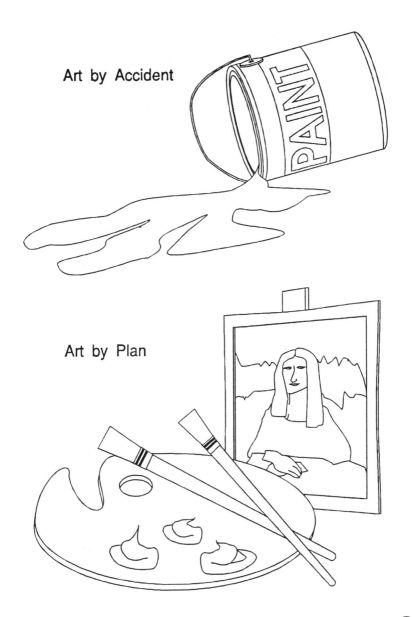

Limitations of Equipment

The human eye and ear are two extraordinary instruments for sensing light and sound, respectively. No human invention has ever come close to matching the capabilities of those two sensory organs. It is easy to forget how limited the electronic aural and visual equipment are until we compare them to their human counterparts.

The human eye can focus from nearly the end of the nose to infinity instantaneously. The eye can adjust to light variations quickly and can pick out images in light varying over a thousand times from the lightest to the darkest. The human ear can hear sounds varying in loudness from 0 decibels to over 160 decibels and can respond to frequency changes from 15 hertz to over 20,000 hertz.

The best video camera cannot reveal detail in light variations greater than 30 to 1, and most consumer cameras have difficulty creating acceptable images beyond 15 to 1. The very best lenses have limited focus range, and the depth of field depends on the amount of light present and focal length and f-stop settings. The best microphone is limited to less than 60 decibels loudness range, and most audio equipment cannot reproduce frequencies without inconsistent variations beyond a range of 10,000 hertz.

It is important to remember that the audio/video equipment is converting sound and light to electronic impulses and that, regardless of the expense or quality of the equipment used, it cannot capture everything that the human eye and ear can. The limitations of the equipment therefore play a crucial role in the planning of a video production.

SUPERIORITY OF HUMAN SENSES

The human eye reproduces
over 1000:1 ratio of light to dark

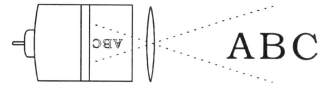

The best video camera reproduces
30:1 ratio of light to dark

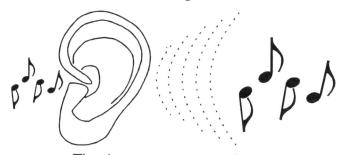

The human ear reproduces
sounds as loud as 160 decibals

The best microphones reproduce
sounds no louder than 60 decibals

The Audio Signal: Frequency

The audio signal may be considered to have two basic characteristics: frequency (tone) and amplitude (loudness). In order to create with and record sound these two characteristics must be understood.

Frequency is measured in hertz or cycles per second and is abbreviated Hz. Since most of the sound humans can hear is above 1,000 hertz, the abbreviation kHz, or kilohertz, is often used since *k* is the abbreviation for *kilo*, the metric equivalent of 1,000.

A *cycle* is the time or distance between peaks of a single sound vibration. A single continuous frequency is called a *tone* and is often used for testing. Humans perceive frequency as *pitch*, the highness and lowness of tones. The term *timbre* is a musical term often used in media production that refers to the special feeling a sound may have as a result of its source. For example, a note struck on the piano may be the same frequency as that of the same note played on a trumpet, but the timbre is very different.

The energy spectrum ranges from 0 Hz to above a gigahertz (1 billion hertz). The frequency range most humans can hear falls between 15 Hz and 20 kHz. Frequencies above the audible human range include radio frequencies (RF) used as broadcast carrier waves, microwaves, X rays and light, or the visible spectrum.

Most videotape recorders can record only those audio frequencies between 30 Hz and 10 kHz. The frequencies excluded are not generally missed unless the production requires a wide range of frequency response, such as a music session.

The range of frequency response and certain portions of frequencies may be modified as needed for an individual production. This altering of the frequency response is called *equalization.* When you adjust the tone controls, treble or bass, on a stereo, you are equalizing the signal by modifying the frequency response. Although most videotape recorders do not have equalization controls, some audio mixers and microphones do.

THE ELECTROMAGNETIC FREQUENCY SPECTRUM

Frequency		Description	Range
	10 Hz	Audible Sound	20 Hz - 20 KHz
		A/C Power	50 Hz - 60 Hz
	100 Hz	Maritime Communication	
Kilo	1 KHz	RADIO FREQUENCIES	100 Hz - 100 GHz
	10 KHz	Aircraft Communication	
	100 KHz		
Mega	1 MHz	AM Radio	535 KHz-1065 KHz
		Aircraft, Maritime Communication	1.6 MHz - 50 MHz
		Radar Shortwave Communication	
	10 MHz	VHF Channels 2-6	50 MHz - 88 MHz
		FM Radio	88 MHz - 108 MHz
	100 MHz	VHF TV Channels 7-13	108 MHz-174 MHz
		Military	174 MHz-216 MHz
		UHF TV Channels 14-83	216 MHz-470 MHz
Giga	1 GHz	Mobile, Cellular, Microwave, MDS	470 MHz-12 GHz
	10 GHz	Weather Satellite, Police Radar	12 GHz- 14 GHz
		K-Band Satellite, DBS, Space Satellites	14 GHz-20 GHz
	100 GHz		
Tera	1 THz	Infrared	1 THz - 1,250 THz
	10 THz	HEAT	
	100 THz		
	1,000 THz		
		Visible Light	1,250 THz - 2,500 THz
	10,000 THz	Ultraviolet Light	2,500 THz - 5,000,000 THz
	100,000 THz	X-rays	100,000 THz—
	1,000,000 THz		
	10,000,000 THz		
	100,000,000 THz	Gamma Rays	100,000,000 THz—

The Audio Signal: Amplitude

Amplitude is the energy level of the audio signal. The listener perceives of amplitude as loudness. Relative amplitude is referred to as *level* and is measured in decibels, abbreviated as *dB*. *Deci-* is one tenth on the metric scale, and the *Bell* was the measure of audio amplitude created by Alexander Graham Bell. Because the Bell is a very large unit of measure, the dB is more commonly used. The decibel is a somewhat confusing unit of measurement because it is a reference measurement of the change of the power of the signal. It is not an absolute measurement and is logarithmic, not linear, and can be expressed in either volts or watts. A change of at least 3 dB is necessary in order for the human ear to perceive a change in level.

Volume is the term used when referring to the measurable energy that translates into loudness and may be measured in either volume units (VU) or dB's. Humans are sensitive to a change in volume, but human hearing is not linear. At some frequencies and at some volume levels, the ear senses a change but the actual measure of change is not registered accurately within the human brain. Since no analog audio equipment can handle a volume change greater than approximately 60 dB, accurate level readings must be available during recording to avoid distorted or noisy sound. *Distortion* is an unwanted change in the audio signal. The most common distortion is caused by attempting to record the audio at a level too high for the equipment. If the audio level is too low, noise will be introduced into the audio. *Noise* is unwanted sound added to the audio. Noise is most often created when the audio is recorded at too low of a level.

METRIC TERMS AND
FREQUENCY RESPONSE CURVE

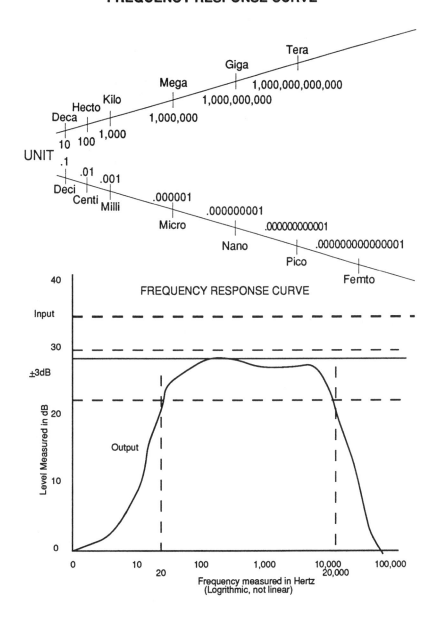

Measuring Audio

The audio level can be measured as it is being recorded by using a VU meter, a peak to peak meter, or light emitting diodes (LED). Each of these gives the operator an indication of the level of the audio. When the level is too high, the meters will read above the 0 dB indicator, and with LEDs, the color of the flashing diodes will indicate respective level. When the level is too low, the meter needles will barely move, and few, if any, diodes will flash.

The audio operator attempts to keep dynamic levels within the 60 dB range of equipment by *attenuating* the level (bringing it down) when the audio source is too loud and *boosting* the level (bringing it up) when the audio source level is too low. This is called *riding gain* and may be done either manually by the operator or automatically by circuits built into the equipment called *automatic gain controls* (AGC) or *automatic level controls* (ALC).

Dynamics refers to the difference between the loudest and the quietest passage. Most analog equipment is limited to a range of approximately 60 dB; newer digital equipment features dynamic ranges greater than 100 dB.

To achieve the highest possible audio quality, record and reproduce sound as close to the original as possible. Even though it is not possible to record all frequencies at the exact same level as the original sound occurred, a successful operator makes the effort to exclude all noise and avoid distorting the audio signal.

CYCLE AND LOUDNESS CURVES

One Complete Cycle

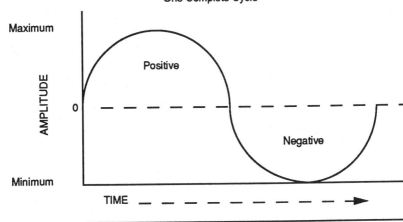

ROBINSON-DADSON LOUDNESS CURVES

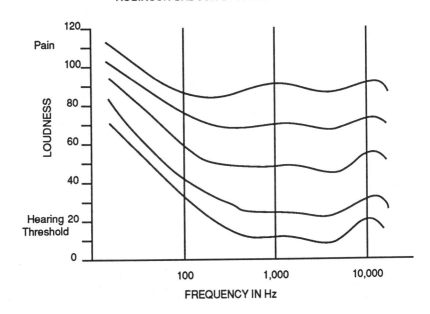

The Video Signal

The video signal, like the audio signal, is made up of voltages varying in frequency and level. Even though the video electronic signal is very complex, you should consider it in much the same manner as the audio signal. The camera cannot record all that the eye can see, nor can a videotape recorder process all the information fed into it. Avoid both video distortion and noise as vehemently as audio distortion and noise.

Video distortion and noise are defined in much the same way as audio distortion and noise, except that you can see video distortion as flare in brightly lit areas, as tearing, or as color shifts in the picture. Video noise can be seen as a grainy or "crawly" texture to the picture.

Changing Light into Electrons

The process of changing light into electrons is a transducing process involving two major changes in energy. The first is the collection and concentration of light reflected from the subject onto the surface of the instrument that changes the light to electrons, and the second is the transforming of that light to an electronic signal.

The three primary functions of a video camera lens are

- to collect as much light reflected from the subject as possible
- to control how much light passes through the lens
- to focus the image on the photosensitive surface of the camera

The secondary function is to provide a certain field of view, either with a fixed-focal-length (prime) lens or with a variable-focal-length (zoom) lens.

The *field of view* is best thought of as the area the camera can see in any one shot. Explanations of optics and the specifics of lens operations and characteristics are covered in the next section.

Light concentrated by the lens onto the surface of the transducer is transformed into electronics by either camera tubes or solid state image sensors. Both processes are complex, but the basic knowledge necessary to properly operate video cameras is not that difficult to acquire.

As the light strikes the surface of the camera tube, the scan beam is altered in proportion to the intensity of the light falling on that specific part of the light sensitive surface. The brighter the light, the greater the reaction. The lower the light, the lesser the reaction.

In the past few years, a new method of converting light into an electronic signal has been developed that is practical for use in both consumer and professional cameras. This is the use of a light sensitive solid-state device known as a *metal oxide semiconductor*, or MOS chip. This chip also is called a *charge-coupled device* (CCD). The chip is small, less than 1 inch square and less than 1/8 inch thick. It operates on much lower voltages and does not burn, streak, or lag, as do camera tubes.

CHANGING LIGHT
INTO ELECTRONS

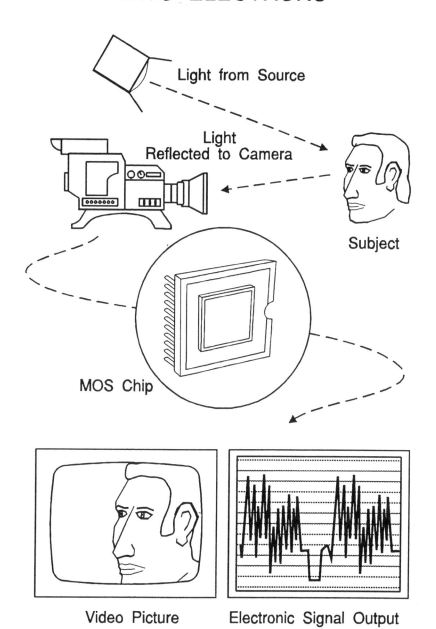

Light from Source

Light
Reflected to Camera

Subject

MOS Chip

Video Picture

Electronic Signal Output

The Scanning System and Synchronization

Scanning System

In order to reproduce the changes in light converted to electronics, a system had to be devised to create a changing light in the TV receiver that matched that of the camera. This was accomplished through the use of a scanning system in the receiver that matched the one in the camera. A beam of electrons starts scanning the inside face of the camera tube and the inside face of the picture tube in the receiver at the same time. Completely scanning the frame, called a *raster*, requires 525 lines, 262.5 at a time, in a pattern called a *field*. The second 262.5 lines scanned are slightly offset from the first set in a pattern called *interlaced scanning*. The total scanning of the two 262.5-line fields is one 525-line frame that occurs once every 1/30 second.

This line-scanning system also operates in the receiver in the same manner so that the picture can be duplicated exactly as originally shot in the camera. Knowledge about the scanning system is not crucial to video production except that the camera operator must be aware that the reproduction system is not based on complete coverage of the field, but instead a series of 525 horizontal lines that make reproducing fine horizontal lines in a picture nearly impossible. The scan system also limits the vertical resolution power of the video system.

Synchronization

In order to be able to reproduce the picture on the home receiver exactly as it was shot in the camera, the signal must contain a component that will keep the lines and frames in synchronization; that is, the scan line in the receiver must start at precisely the same time as the picture is being scanned in the camera, and a new frame must start exactly at the same time as the new frame is started in the camera. This timing sequence is critical and involves very small fractions of time. Each frame lasts 1/30 second; each field lasts 1/60 second; and a new line starts every 1/15,700 second.

In order for this complex system to stay in synchronization, pulses are added between the fields and between the lines. These are called *sync pulses*, and they must be created either in the camera or in a sync generator. The sync pulses are part of the recorded signal and the receiver locks onto those pulses when the tape is played back. The pulses can be corrected if there are errors in their timing by running the signal through a time base corrector (TBC).

14

NTSC SCAN SYSTEM

Two-field, One-frame Interlace System

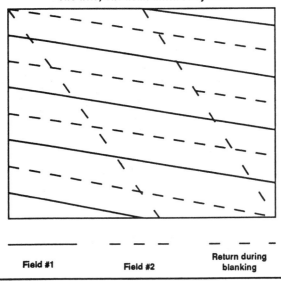

Field #1	Field #2	Return during blanking

ELECTRONIC SIGNAL OF TWO FIELDS AS SEEN ON THE FACE OF A WAVEFORM MONITOR (Oscilloscope)

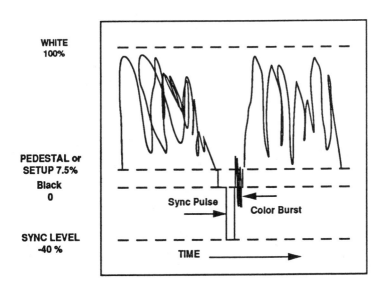

WHITE
100%

PEDESTAL or
SETUP 7.5%
Black
0

SYNC LEVEL
-40 %

Sync Pulse

Color Burst

TIME

Color Video

Previous discussion in this section has focused only on the black-and-white, or *luminance*, characteristic of the video signal. In order to create and reproduce a color signal, the other characteristic of light, the *chrominance* or color portion, must be addressed. The 525-line system was agreed upon early in the history of the development of television in this country by a committee called the National Television Standards Committee (NTSC). In 1941 (just before World War II), equipment that could be manufactured at a reasonable cost could accommodate no more than 525 lines. In the near future that standard may be altered as discussions continue toward the development of High Density Television (HDTV), a higher resolution system utilizing more lines and a wider scan ratio.

Following World War II, NTSC decided that the best method of adding color to the black-and-white television of that time was to use an all electronic system. Mechanical systems and noncompatible systems with more scan lines have been suggested, but would potentially render all existing television production equipment and receivers obsolete. Instead, NTSC recommended the adoption of the RCA-compatible system.

The RCA system separated the light entering the camera into the three primary additive colors—red, green, and blue—by using filters and three camera tubes. That created three signals: a red signal, a green signal, and a blue signal. These three signals were then combined into one signal, but each of the separate color components was placed out of phase so they could be separated later at the receiver. Out of phase signals are related signals on a common path that are shifted slightly in time so they may be kept separate in processing.

The color receiver has only one picture tube; the three streams of electrons strike the face of the picture tube, which is coated with groupings of dots of the three colors. When the three separate signals from the camera are fed to the three separate guns in the receiver, the original color is reproduced by the relative brightness of the three different colors of dots.

This originally meant the color cameras and all color equipment were much larger, much bulkier, and much more expensive to manufacture and operate than existing black-and-white equipment. However, with the appearance of solid-state electronics, and especially the MOS chips that replaced camera tubes, color equipment has become smaller, higher in quality, less expensive, and easier to operate than the black-and-white equipment of 15 years ago.

TV OPTICAL SYSTEMS

Light passes through lens to video transducers
(either tube or chips)

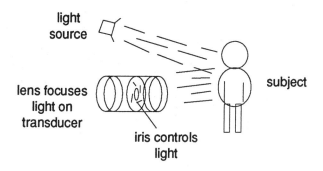

light
source

lens focuses
light on
transducer

iris controls
light

subject

color-separating prism

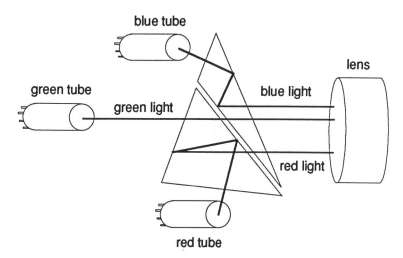

blue tube

green tube

green light

blue light

lens

red light

red tube

Prisms and special reflective coatings make colored light
separate into three primary colors for conversion to electronics

Measuring Video

In order to determine exactly how the camera is reacting to the light reflected from the subject, you need a precise means of looking at the electronic signal. The equivalent of an audio VU meter, a test instrument called an *oscilloscope*, or *waveform monitor*, is used to monitor a black-and-white video signal. It converts the electronic signal into a visual equivalent that is calibrated for precise measurement. The scope can be set to look at one or two lines or at one or two fields at a time.

This electronic picture shows the sync pulses, their amplitude, their width, and their position in relation to other parts of the signal. It also shows the strength or level of the signal to indicate if the signal is too high (too much video amplifier gain or too much light coming into the lens) or too low (too little gain or not enough light). It also shows the relationship between the two major components of the signal: *gain* (white level) and *setup* (black level), sometimes called *pedestal*. These two signals must remain in the proper relative strength to each other to provide an acceptable picture.

In most newer cameras, the white level and black level are set automatically but may need to be adjusted periodically by a technician. The white level is controlled also by the iris setting in the lens. The ability to read and understand an oscilloscope is necessary only during a multiple-camera shoot and in the editing room.

The second type of video-signal monitor is a *vectorscope*. It shows the relationship of the three color signals: red, green, and blue. These three signals are deliberately set out of phase with each other; that is, each of the three start at slightly different times (in fractions of microseconds). This out-of-phase condition is very critical in converting the three black-and-white signals into one acceptable color signal. In order to make that adjustment, it is necessary to read a vectorscope, which visually displays the phase relationships of the three signals. Once again, this is an internal adjustment in most field cameras, and the ability to read and use a vectorscope becomes necessary only with multiple-camera productions and in the editing room.

18

WAVEFORM MONITOR
AND VECTORSCOPE

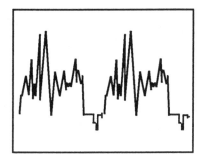

Waveform Monitor
(oscilliscope)

Electronic equivalent of
black/white (luminance value)

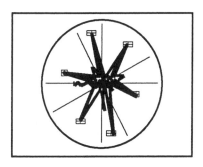

Vectorscope

Electronic equivalent of
color (chrominance and saturation values)

International Video Standards

In 1941, NTSC set the 525-line, 30-frame interlaced system for black-and-white television in this country. In 1954, they set the color standard with the design of the out-of-phase system that maintained compatibility for black-and-white sets as well as color sets. The compatible system meant that a color signal carried both luminance and chrominance signals. On a black-and-white set, the color signal looked like a black-and-white signal, but full color was visible on a color set. At the same time, a color set would reproduce a black-and-white signal in black and white as if the set were a black-and-white receiver.

Following World War II, the rest of the world began to set their standards, but by then technology had advanced well beyond the 525-line standard set in this country. In addition, most other countries used power based on a 50-Hz-per-second rate, rather than the U.S. system of 60 Hz. Two major non-NTSC-compatible systems emerged. In 1961, Phase Alternating Line (PAL) was developed in England. PAL uses a 625-line 25-frame rate and is considered to be superior in color reproduction to NTSC.

In 1967, the French put into service the Sequential Color with Memory (SECAM), an 819-line system, considered superior to both NTSC and PAL. The major problem with these three systems is not their difference in quality, but the fact that they are incompatible; that is, a program originated in an NTSC camera and/or recorded on an NTSC recorder cannot be viewed on either a PAL or SECAM receiver or played back on either a PAL or SECAM recorder.

With the advent of satellites, the expansion of world travel, and the interchange of communication, this incompatibility means that if you are traveling in a non-NTSC country with your American camcorder, you cannot play back your recordings on a local tape or view them on a local receiver. It also means that a signal broadcast from Germany cannot be viewed in France and that if you move from England to the United States, you must leave behind all of your video equipment, including your television receiver. Standards conversion equipment is available, but the equipment is expensive and some loss in signal quality occurs during the conversion.

INTERNATIONAL VIDEO STANDARDS

NTSC

Bahamas
Barbados
Bermuda
Bolivia
Canada
Chile
Colombia
Costa Rica
Cuba
Curacao
Dominican Republic
Ecuador
El Salvador
Guam
Guatemala
Hawaii
Honduras
Japan
South Korea
Mexico
Nicaragua
Panama
Peru
Phillipines
Puerto Rico
Taiwan
Trinidad & Tobago
USA
Venezuela
Virgin Islands

SECAM

Albania
Bulgaria
Congo
Czechoslovakia
Egypt
France
*Dem.Rep. Germany
Greece
Haiti
Hungary
Iran
Iraq
Lebanon
Libya
Luxembourg
Monaco
Mongolia
Morocco
Poland
Rumania
Saudi Arabia
Syria
Tunisia
USSR

PAL

Afghanistan
Algeria
Andorra
Angola
Argentina
Australia
Austria
Azores
Bahrain
Bangladesh
Belgium
Brazil (M)
Ceylon
Peoples Rep.China
Denmark
Finland
*Federal Rep. Germany
Gibraltar
Great Britain
Hong Kong
Iceland
India
Ireland
Isreal
Jamaica
Jordan
Kenya
North Korea
Malaysia
Mozambique
Netherlands
New Zealand
Nigeria
Norway
Pakistan
Paraguay
Portugal
Singapore
South Africa
Spain
Sudan
Sweden
Switzerland
Thailand
Turkey
Uganda
Uruguay
Yugoslavia

* With the reunification of Germany,
a choice will be made between the
two system now in use. PAL probably
will be the logical choice.

Background

The equipment presently used in single-camera video production has a relatively short history. In the early 1960s, a method of editing quadraplex videotape was developed. It occurred to directors and newspeople that some types of productions could be shot on one camera, recorded on videotape, even out of sequence, and then edited into a form suitable for airing. The first attempts used the bulky and complex black-and-white image orthicon cameras and 2-inch videotape equipment. The method was not particularly practical except for those rare events, usually news stories, that lent themselves to this type of production.

By 1967, amateur videotaping became possible with the invention and sale of a Sony black-and-white vidicon hand-held camera combined with an open reel 1/2-inch videotape recorder, later known as the *EIAJ format*. The early attempts at single-camera video production were very primitive, primarily because of the lack of an adequate and efficient editing system for either 2-inch quad or EIAJ 1/2-inch formats.

In the late 1970s, editing systems for both formats were developed, but the marketing of Beta and VHS 1/2-inch and 3/4-inch U-matic videocassette formats superceded the use of 2-inch and 1/2-inch EIAJ. The 2-inch format was difficult to edit, even with a computer controller, because it could not be still-framed for precise location of edit points, and the quality of 1/2-inch EIAJ was below the technical level warranting the further development of editing systems.

The original small-field cameras were developed for broadcast news operations to replace the 16mm film equipment used by most stations and networks. News operations wanted small, lightweight equipment that could deliver broadcast quality picture and sound instantaneously. Since such a system would be all-electronic, the picture and sound also could be transmitted over microwave links for live coverage. Such coverage was first successfully tried by CBS in 1974, using a small camera and an early portable 1-inch helical videotape recorder. These early news cameras (called *creepy-peepies*) as well as the first consumer video cameras used a single vidicon picture tube that created a black-and-white picture. The equipment was bulky and heavy compared to film equipment, but it did provide the live picture requested by news.

24

EARLY EFP EQUIPMENT

Early Remote Van
with Microwave Dish
and Studio Camera

Early "Creepy-Peepy"
with Back Pack and
Hand-Held SONY
Black-&-White Vidicon
Camera

The Image Source: Tubes

Until the late 1980s all practical video cameras used an electronic tube to convert light to an electronic signal. The early cameras used a combination of image orthicon (IO) and a variety of different types of vidicon tubes manufactured by various companies under such brand names as Saticon, Plumbicon, and others. The process of converting light to an electronic signal in all of the tubes was basically the same.

The original IO tubes were as large as 4 inches in diameter and 18 inches in length; the latest vidicon tubes are as small as 1/2 inch in diameter and 5 inches in length. The decrease in the size of the tube permitted the development of smaller cameras requiring less power to operate, all of which decreased the overall size of the camera. At the same time, the quality of the picture improved as better circuits and components were developed.

Even though the quality and size of the tube cameras made them more applicable to both news operations and consumer use, the fact that they used tubes as light conversion transducers presented problems. The most critical was their low level of light sensitivity as compared to film. The average three-tube color camera has an equivalent ASA, or light sensitivity, of about 12 to 25. Today's film stocks are now rated as high as ASA 1000, allowing cinematography in light levels far below what a videographer must have in order to produce an acceptable picture.

The second crucial aspect of tubes was their susceptibility to "burn," lag, and/or bloom. When a tube camera was pointed at a bright high contrast light source, such as the sun or a spotlight on stage, the surface of the tube was damaged so that it would not accurately respond to normal light. In fact, it produced a color on the opposite side of the color chart: a blue subject looked yellow where the tube was burned. If the camera was panned across a bright image, a negative image trailed (lagged) behind the original. Blooming appeared as a dark halo around objects that sharply contrasted with their background.

The third problem inherent in tube cameras was their sensitivity to loss of registration. Since the picture produced was actually three pictures created by the three different tubes, the tubes had to be precisely and accurately aligned, or *registered*, in order to reproduce an accurate reproduction of the original subject. Any bumping or jarring of the camera tended to knock at least one tube out of registration, requiring a technician to reregister the camera before it could be used again.

INTERNAL PARTS OF A CAMERA TUBE

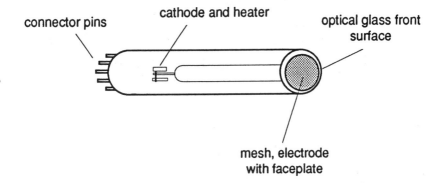

connector pins

cathode and heater

optical glass front surface

mesh, electrode with faceplate

The heart of the chip camera, the CCD (charge-coupled device)sensor.

27

The Image Source: Chips

In 1984, RCA in America and NEC in Japan marketed the first video camera that contained no tubes. The light conversion tubes were replaced with all-electronic charge coupled devices (CCD). These CCDs (known as *chips*) are flat pieces of selenium and other light-sensitive metal crystal pixels. Instead of using a beam of electrons to scan the chip, the new technology uses a chip that is electronically read as light falling across its surface changes voltages and currents. These changes become the electronic equivalent of the picture at the same frame and line rate as a picture tube.

The chips require a very small amount of power compared to even the smallest camera tubes, and since they are a flat piece of metal, they may be mounted directly to the surface of the light-splitting prisms inside the camera. This avoids any changes in registration between the chips, thus making the camera more rugged. The chips also are not prone to "burning" or aging as tubes are. However, the chips are more prone to streaking when panned across a bright light source, and vertical objects may appear to bend during a pan. The technology for compensating for these characteristics now exists for chip cameras.

Since the chips are solid-state components just like transistors, they last as long as any other component in the camera. In tube cameras the tubes had to be replaced periodically as they lost sensitivity and were damaged from burning. The cost for replacement often nearly equaled the original cost of the camera.

TUBES AND CHIPS

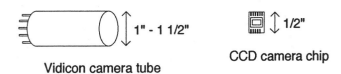

1" - 1 1/2"

Vidicon camera tube

CCD camera chip

1/2"

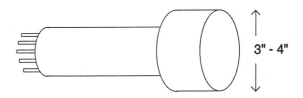

3" - 4"

Image orthicon camera tube

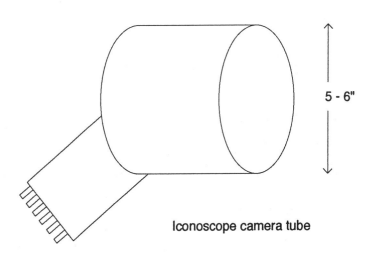

5 - 6"

Iconoscope camera tube

Light Gathering: Optics and Focal Length

In order for a camera to operate, it must contain a means of concentrating light reflected from the surface of subjects in order to create an image. In today's cameras, this function is provided by the *lens*, a series of optical glass or plastic elements cemented together and mounted in such a way as to focus light on the surface of the light conversion tubes or chips.

The lens is mounted permanently on the front of a consumer-quality camera. In equipment used at the professional level, interchangeable lenses may be used. The three basic characteristics of a lens are its focal length, its focus range, and its aperture settings.

Focal Length

The *focal length* of a lens is a measurement of the ratio between the diameter of the lens and the distance from its optical center to the focal plane (the location of the tube or chip faces), usually given in millimeters. The important factor to remember about focal length is that the longer the measurement, the greater the enlargement of the subject; the shorter the measurement, the smaller the subject will appear. Conversely, the longer focal length allows space for fewer subjects in the frame, and the shorter focal length allows more subjects to be included in the frame.

In addition, the longer the focal length, the more compressed the distance appears going away from the camera (called the *Z* axis). Also, movement in front of the camera (the *X* axis) will appear to be accelerated. The apparent distances on the *Z* axis using a short-focal-length lens will appear to be increased, and movement on the *X* axis will appear to be slowed down. Other characteristics of lenses determined by the focal length will be explained later in this section.

FOCAL LENGTH

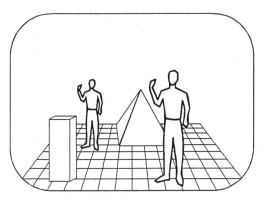

Long Focal Length:
subjects enlarged, fewer subjects in frame,
compressed appearance of distance

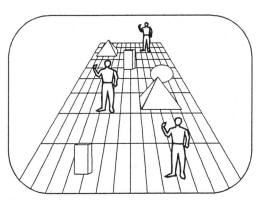

Short Focal Length:
subjects smaller, more subjects in frame,
increased appearance of distance

Focus and Aperture

Focus

The ability of the lens to concentrate light reflected from a subject to create the sharpest image is called *focus*. *Focus* is a relative term since a lens is in focus on an image when that image appears as sharply and clearly as possible on the surface of the picture tube or chips. There are two separate methods of focusing an image, both of which must be accurately set in order to achieve that sharp image.

The most obvious is called the *front focus*. It is achieved by adjusting (usually by turning the barrel of the lens) until the image is sharply focused at a point behind the lens called the *focal point*. The second focus is the *back focus*, which involves adjusting either the lens body or the pickup surface until an image located an infinite distance from the camera is in focus on the surface of the tubes/chips. The back focus is a technician's adjustment and should not have to be readjusted unless the camera or lens is jarred or bumped out of adjustment.

Focusing a zoom lens is more complex than focusing a prime or fixed-focal-length lens. The lens must be zoomed to its maximum focal length, framed and focused on the intended subject, and then zoomed back to the desired framing. All subjects located the same distance from the camera as the original subject will be in focus. Shooting any subject closer or further away from the camera will require resetting the focus.

Aperture

The third basic characteristic of a lens is its *aperture* or iris setting. In order to better control the amount of light that strikes the surface of the tubes or chips, an *iris* or variable opening is built into the lens. In the early days of photography, a numbering system was developed that is still in use today—not only in photography, but also in cinematography and videography.

The carefully calibrated sizes of the opening in the aperture are labeled with numbers called *f-stops*. Although the numbering system seems strange, each full stop doubles (if opening) or halves (if closing) the amount of light allowed to pass through the lens. The number is the ratio of the focal length to the diameter of the aperture opening. The common full f-stops used in videography are f-1.4, 2, 2.8, 4, 5.6, 8, 11, 16, and 22. One of the confusing aspects of f-stops is that as the number increases in size, the aperture opening decreases, allowing less light to pass through the lens. The converse is also true: The smaller the f-stop the more light passes through the lens. In addition, the term *stop down* means to close the aperture, or increase the f-stop number; to *open up* means to increase the size of the aperture opening but lower the f-stop number.

FRONT FOCUS - BACK FOCUS

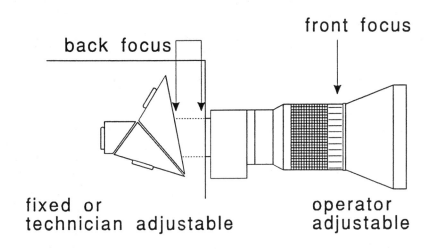

back focus

front focus

fixed or
technician adjustable

operator
adjustable

F-STOP OPENINGS

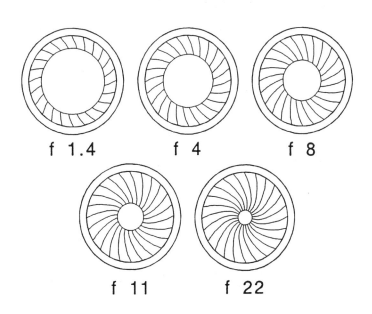

f 1.4   f 4   f 8

f 11   f 22

Depth of Field

Each of the previous characteristics of the lens—focal length (FL), focus, and f-stops—are tools to use in controlling the image desired by the videographer. Focal length affects how many subjects, how much of the subject, and the size of the subject in the frame. It also alters the appearance of subjects by distorting their size as mentioned earlier in this section.

Focus directs the attention of the viewer by placing important subjects in focus and less important subjects or subjects to be ignored out of focus. Changing the focus, called *rolling* or *pulling focus,* can also guide the attention of the viewer from one subject to another.

The f-stops must be set within the technical limitations of the camera and source of light so that there is enough light for the tubes/chips to create an image and not so much light that either the tubes or chips are overpowered. The mood and apparent time of day can be altered by changing the f-stop. Slight underexposure can give the appearance of evening, early morning, or even nighttime or suggest a gloomy, dramatic mood. Slight overexposure can give the impression of bright daytime or lend a comic, lighthearted feeling.

A fourth characteristic of lenses, depth of field (DOF) is dependent on the three already described. *Depth of field* is the distance from the camera that subjects appear in acceptable focus. This distance is a range dependent upon the focal length of the lens, its focus setting, and the aperture opening. The longer the focal length, the closer the focus point, and the more wide open the aperture setting, the shallower the depth of field. The converse is also true.

Depth of field is critical when trying to focus on close-ups; on rapidly moving subjects, such as in sports; and when light levels are limited. Depth of field also may be used creatively to exclude some subjects by placing them out of focus but within the frame.

DEPTH OF FIELD

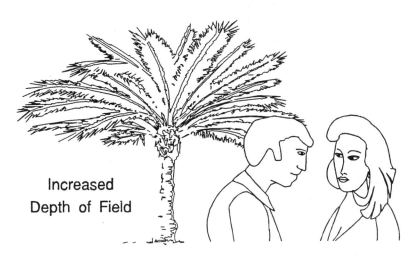

Increased
Depth of Field

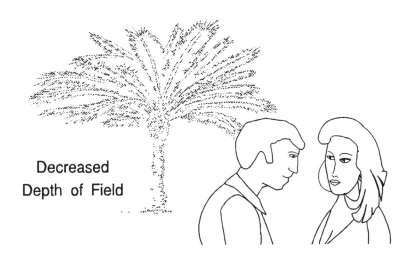

Decreased
Depth of Field

35

Viewfinder

In order for you to see what subjects you have included in your picture frame, you will need an accurate viewfinder designed to accompany the camera. The viewfinder is usually mounted to the camera body so that the camera may be either hand held or tripod mounted.

A *viewfinder* is simply a small video monitor, similar to a home television receiver except that it is wired directly into the camera and does not contain RF circuits to take signals from the air. Most cameras have small signal lights mounted inside the viewfinder hood so that you can monitor the operational characteristics of the camera without taking your eye from the viewfinder.

Most viewfinders are mounted on the left side of the camera, making it difficult for a person who uses the left eye predominately to operate the camera. People who wear eyeglasses also often may experience difficulties in looking into the viewfinder.

The majority of viewfinders include contrast and brightness controls for adjusting the monitor in the viewfinder. These controls should not be adjusted except when the camera is either focused on a well-lit test pattern or is generating an internal test pattern called *color bars*. If adjustments are attempted while shooting anything other than a test pattern, the viewfinder may be incorrectly adjusted in attempting to compensate for a poorly lit subject.

Camera Viewfinder

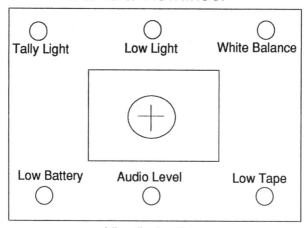

Tally Light Low Light White Balance

Low Battery Audio Level Low Tape

Viewfinder Face

Signal Lights located inside viewfinder face

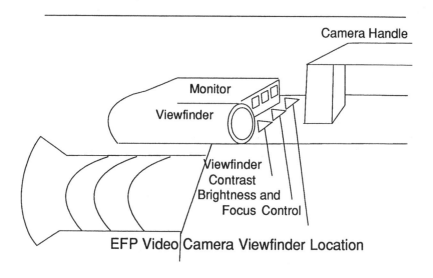

Camera Handle

Monitor

Viewfinder

Viewfinder
Contrast
Brightness and
Focus Control

EFP Video Camera Viewfinder Location

Camera Controls I

Each brand and model of field camera and recorder may have different controls and more than likely different labels for the same controls. The description that follows uses the most common labels for the most common controls. Always consult your operation manual before attempting to operate any piece of equipment as complex as a video camera, despite those salesperson claims that you just "point and shoot."

Bars/Gain Selector

The first control to set is the "bars/gain" selector. Generally the two functions are combined on one control, but on rare occasions they will be separated. When the selector is set to "bars," color test bars will appear in the viewfinder and are the output of the camera. This test signal is necessary to set the controls on the monitor, and you should record 30 seconds to 1 minute of bars at the head of each tape and at the start of each shooting session. This signal will be invaluable later for trouble shooting if there are problems with either the camera or recorder. The "gain" selector, which also may be labeled "sensitivity," provides a variety of increases in video gain should light levels be too low for shooting at the normal gain position. The switch usually is marked with several steps: 6 dB, 9 dB, 18 dB, and so on. Each of these steps provides the equivalent of another f-stop of amplification. The price paid for the use of this control is the increase in video noise as higher gain is used. Video noise appears as a "crawling" on the surface of the picture.

Color Temperature Control/Filter Selector

A "color temperature" control designed to change the filters placed between the lens and the pickup tubes or chips may be labeled "filter selector." It usually is a portion of a wheel that holds a variety of filters and that is accessible from the side or the front of the camera. Turn this wheel to select a particular filter or no filter. The no-filter position is intended for use indoors under incandescent lighting. For outdoor shooting, the filter may be either an 85 (yellow) or 85+ND (Neutral Density) filter designed to add the yellow that is missing from the blue daylight. The ND filter added to the 85 compensates for bright sunlight, which might provide too much light for the video camera.

Besides those two positions, there may be additional filters. There may be both an 85 and an 85+ND or even several choices of different intensities of ND filters. There also may be an FL-M filter (magenta) to help compensate for fluorescent lighting.

Back and Right Side of EFP Camera

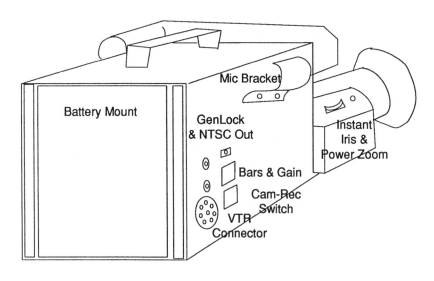

Battery Mount

Mic Bracket

GenLock
& NTSC Out

Instant
Iris &
Power Zoom

Bars & Gain

Cam-Rec
Switch

VTR
Connector

Camera Controls II

White Balance

Once you have chosen the proper color temperature filter to match the lighting under which the shoot is to take place, the camera then must be *white balanced*. To do this the camera is focused on a pure white source, generally a card or the back of a clean T-shirt, and then the "white balance" or "auto white" button is held down for several seconds. Some cameras indicate with a light in the viewfinder when the camera has set the white balance internally; others make you guess when white balance has been reached.

Very simple and inexpensive consumer cameras may not provide any other operator controls. On better cameras, the following controls will be found. A "power selector" switch is used to indicate whether the camera will have a battery mounted on it, be powered with its own separate AC power supply, or will derive its power from the recorder's power supply or battery.

There may be a "VTR selector" switch to enable your camera to operate with a variety of different recorders manufactured by someone other than the manufacturer of your camera. A "VTR start" switch may be mounted on the camera body, but more than likely will be mounted on the lens hand grip close to the thumb for easy use. This switch allows you to start and stop the recorder without leaving the camera or taking your eye from the viewfinder.

The following controls are usually located on the lens or lens mount: Iris mode, iris inst., zoom mode, zoom speed, and zoom control. The "iris mode" control allows you to choose between setting the iris manually or letting the camera's automatic iris circuits set the iris. The "iris inst." control is designed so that you can zoom in on the surface that is reflecting the average amount of light for that scene, such as the face of the subject; press the "iris inst." control, which will lock the iris at that setting; and then zoom back and/or pan to whatever framing is needed or to the beginning of that scene.

The "zoom mode" allows the operator the same option for the zoom lens. Either the operator can zoom the lens manually or use the lens's motorized control to zoom the lens. The zoom lens control is usually a rocker switch that allows you to press one end to zoom in and the other end to zoom out. The harder you press, the faster the lens will zoom. A very gentle touch will produce a slow, smooth zoom.On some cameras an additional control allows you to set the speed range of the zoom control from very slow to very fast.

One additional control may be mounted on either the lens or the camera body. The "return video" or "VTR return" control is a button that, when pressed, feeds the picture being played back from the tape deck into the viewfinder, allowing the videographer to observe the images already recorded.

Location of Controls on front of EFP

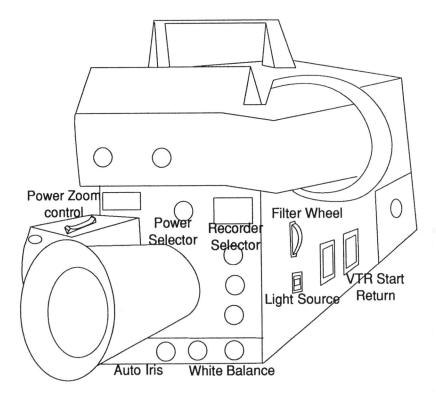

Front and Left Side

Camera Supports: Tripods

One of the first visual characteristics separating novice and professional videographers is the stability of the picture. Although most cameras can be hand held, and most consumer cameras are so small that a tripod seems redundant, a steady, controlled picture is essential for a quality video production.

The standard method of supporting a video camera is on a tripod. The usual tripod has three legs that are collapsible and individually adjustable in length to provide a solid, level support for the tripod head. The head is designed to fasten to the tripod and afford a system of moving the camera back and forth on a horizontal plane, called a *pan*, and up and down, called a *tilt*. In addition, better tripod heads have a provision for precisely leveling the head by means of a leveling bubble built into the tripod.

The heads are manufactured in a variety of designs depending on how expensive and how professional a piece of equipment the videographer requires. The critical factor in the design of heads is the method used to provide enough back pressure or *drag* so that a smooth steady pan or tilt is possible. The method for creating drag separates the amateur tripods from the professional. The least expensive and most common heads for the consumer model tripods are friction heads that develop drag by the friction of two metal or fabric surfaced plates. It is difficult, if not impossible, to pan or tilt smoothly while recording with a friction head.

The next most expensive and higher quality head develops its drag through a set of springs. In some designs with lighter weight cameras, this system works well. The most suitable and expensive is the fluid head. Drag in this type of head is created by the movement of a thick fluid from one chamber to another. This provides the basis for the smoothest and most easily controlled pans and tilts.

CAMERA SUPPORTS

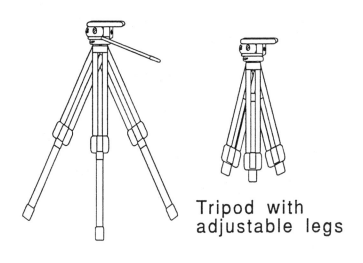

Tripod with adjustable legs

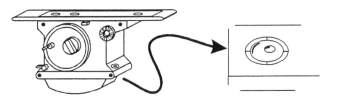

Fluid head with leveling bubble

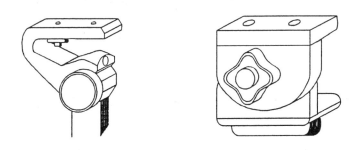

Spring-loaded head   Friction head

Other Camera Support Systems

In the professional world many other support systems are used for single-camera production. Some of them are called *cranes, dollies, crab dollies, pedestals,* and *body mounts.* Most of these systems are expensive, bulky, and physically large. However, they do contribute a wide variety of different potential movements to the director in a production when needed. For a beginner, some of the same camera movements can be created by exploiting simpler pieces of equipment.

One way to move a camera while recording is to add wheels to the tripod, but this is not a very stable or satisfactory method. A wheelchair or grocery cart furnishes a far more stable and easily controlled means of doing dollies and tracking shots. Sitting in a van shooting out of a side or rear door also is a means of getting movement into a sequence. It helps to let a little air out of the tires and place a monitor where it is visible to the driver without being distracting. Warning: Don't try this on a freeway. Hand-holding the camera in a moving vehicle—whether it is an automobile, airplane, helicopter, or boat—absorbs some of the shock and vibration, but the more the camera can be isolated from the movement of the vehicle, the better. Supporting the camera in a harness made of the heavy nylon or rubber bungee cords used by motorcyclists and truck drivers often will yield that type of flexible but vibration-proof support.

To duplicate a 360-degree crane shot, it is possible for the camera operator, camera, and tape deck to ride on a slow moving merry-go-round. A friendly electrician or telephone installer may allow you to ride in the bucket on his crane truck for a high-rising or lowering shot. A fork lift with a platform large enough for a tripod and camera operator will produce a limited pedestal up and/or down shot. Even riding up or down in a glass-sided elevator can supply a long vertical shot.

Professionals use a low mount without tripod legs called a *high hat* to mount the head near the ground or on the hood of an automobile or boat. One method of duplicating this effect is to clamp the head to a heavy board, such as a short length of two-by-twelve. This board then is set either on the ground or clamped to the hood or deck. A safety rope is a necessity for this type of operation.

MOVEABLE CAMERA MOUNTS

Studio Crane

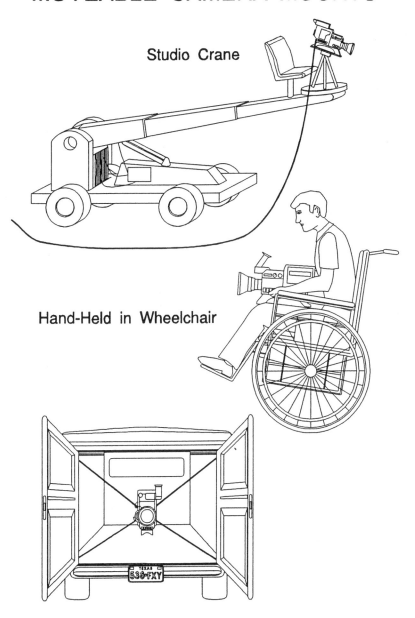

Hand-Held in Wheelchair

Slung on Bungee Cords

Hand-holding the Camera

Many beginners and family videographers feel constrained by mounting the camera on a tripod or any other support. A much better production is possible with a stable support, but for those who cannot or will not use a tripod, here are some helpful hints on hand-holding a camera.

The first rule is to replace the tripod with your body, even though the body is only a bipod and a fairly unsteady one at that. By leaning against a third support to create a tripod the unsteadiness of hand-holding can be minimized. Lean against a wall, a post, an automobile, a building, or any other stable support to steady yourself.

Hold the camera firmly on your shoulder, with the elbows held tightly against the rib cage. Do not try to hold the camera away from the body except when holding it over your head to shoot over a crowd, between your legs to duplicate a low-angle shot, or under your arm. The position that provides an even steadier platform than trying to hold the camera on the shoulder is one in which the camera is held under the right arm. This works only if the lower camera angle is not improper for that shot and is only possible if the camera's viewfinder may be swiveled up so that you can look down into it.

If a "walking shot" is attempted, remember that the body mounts are designed around gyroscopes that keep the camera pointed in one direction and level at all times. This gyro effect may be partially duplicated by using the body effectively. Hold the camera on the shoulder or under an arm, watch through the viewfinder, and move stiff-legged, swinging the body weight from one leg to the other. The swinging motion must be compensated for by swinging the camera an equal amount in the opposite direction so that it is always pointed at the subject. If the shot is supposed to be the point of view (POV) of someone walking, then the slight weaving and bobbing is acceptable. If not, much practice will be necessary to make a smooth "dolly" while hand-holding the camera.

When panning with the camera, place the feet in a comfortable position at the FINISH of the pan. Then twist the body into the starting position. This unwinding effect allows the body to relax as it approaches the end of the pan, instead of building tension and the shakes that go with such tension. This same technique works somewhat the same in a lengthy tilt. Position the body in a comfortable position at end of the tilt, not at the beginning.

Remember, the human body was never meant to hand-hold a camera, and only through much practice and physical conditioning can a reasonably satisfactory shot be achieved by hand-holding.

HAND-HELD CAMERA POSITIONS

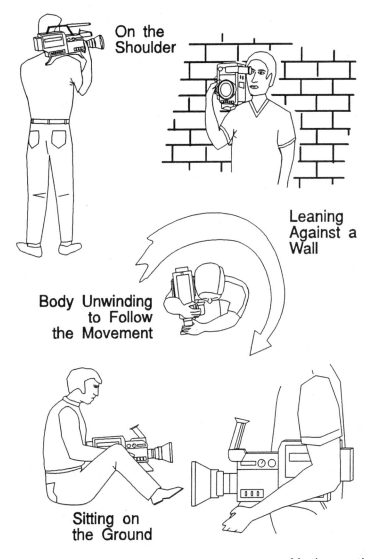

On the Shoulder

Leaning Against a Wall

Body Unwinding to Follow the Movement

Sitting on the Ground

Underneath the Arm

Video Recording

The VCR's function, whether as a separate unit from the camera or attached to the camera making a complete unit or camcorder, is to store the electronic impulses that represent the sound and picture created by the camera. This storage must be in such a manner that the impulses may be easily retrieved in as close to their original form as possible. The recorder's ability to accurately reproduce the original signal is tied directly to the cost of the equipment.

The physical and electronic components designed to record and play back the video and audio signals have been refined over the past 30 years to an amazing level of quality for an equally amazing level of cost.

As the video and audio signals pass from the camera to the recorder, the audio signal is fed to a recording head similar to the recording head on an audio tape recorder. It is in a fixed position and the audio signal is recorded in a longitudinal or continuous path on the edge of the tape stock.

On the opposite edge of the tape a signal generated inside the camera, called the *control track*, is also recorded using a fixed longitudinal track.

Because the video signal is a much more complex signal, recorded at much higher frequencies than either the audio or the control track signal, a different method of recording must be used. In order to record the high video frequencies, the relative speed of the record head passing the tape must be at a much higher speed than it is practical to record in a longitudinal or straight-line manner. Instead, the tape is wrapped around a drum containing one or more video recording heads that rotate inside the drum in the opposite direction from that taken by the tape as it is moving around the drum. The video heads barely project from the drum, touching the tape just enough to record the video signal in a series of slanted tracks across the tape. The tape is wrapped around the head in a helical shape which is the source of one of the two common names for this type of recording: *helical recording*. The other term is *slant track*, an obvious reference to the pattern of video laid down on the tape.

Each video track contains all of the signals necessary for one field, so that if the tape deck is paused at any point, whichever field is wrapped around the drum will be visible as the output of the recorder. In the pause position audio cannot be heard, and control track pulses cannot be counted because the tape must be moving across the playback heads for these two signals to be reproduced.

Since it takes two fields to make a complete frame, when the picture is in pause it is not an accurate reproduction of the recorded signal but it is sufficiently clear for editing purposes.

48

VIDEO RECORDING HEADS

Location of VCR Recording Heads

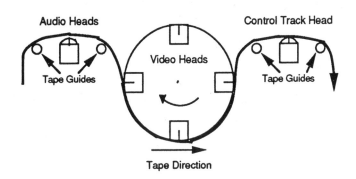

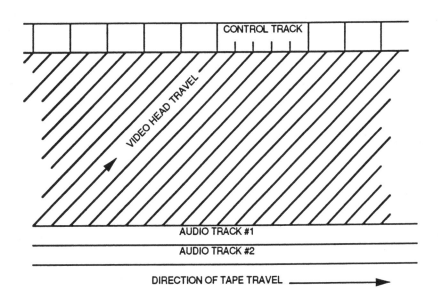

3/4 " U-Matic Signal Tracks

Videotape Stock

The videocassette recorder (VCR), as opposed to the videotape recorder (VTR), is designed to record video and audio material on magnetic tape encased in a cassette, rather than spooled onto an open reel. The cassette was developed not only for the convenience of the user but also as a means of protecting the sensitive surface of the tape stock from wrinkling, dirt, oil, and other contaminants, such as hair or smoke particles. The major disadvantage of confining the tape totally inside a cassette is that it makes splicing the tape for either editing or repair purposes difficult, if not impossible.

New blank tape purchased for recording is called *stock* and comes in a variety of forms and lengths, depending on the tape format used. There is very little difference between brand names of new tape stocks, but there are some slight differences in quality depending on the type of tape, whether it is high quality (HQ) in 1/2-inch, broadcast quality in 3/4-inch, or others. There is no difference between tape used for black-and-white and that for color recording. The length of tape purchased should depend on how the tape is going to be used. Shorter tapes make for easier editing; longer tapes are necessary in order to record an entire program on one tape. Since the majority of the cost of the tape stock is the cassette itself, the difference in cost between a 5-minute cassette and a 20-minute cassette is not very much.

It is important to handle cassettes carefully. Even though the tape is protected inside the cassette, care must be taken to keep from exposing the tape to smoke, dust, dirt, moisture, or excessive heat and humidity. Cassettes should always be carried in their cases and stored in their cases in a temperature- and humidity-controlled environment.

As soon as material is recorded on a tape, both the cassette and the case should be clearly labeled indicating the name of the contents, its length, and the date recorded. Taking care of such details early in the recording process will avoid major problems later. It also will provide a means of preventing unwanted recorded tape from occupying storage space and will prevent critical footage from being accidentally destroyed.

VIDEOTAPE AND VIDEO CASSETTES

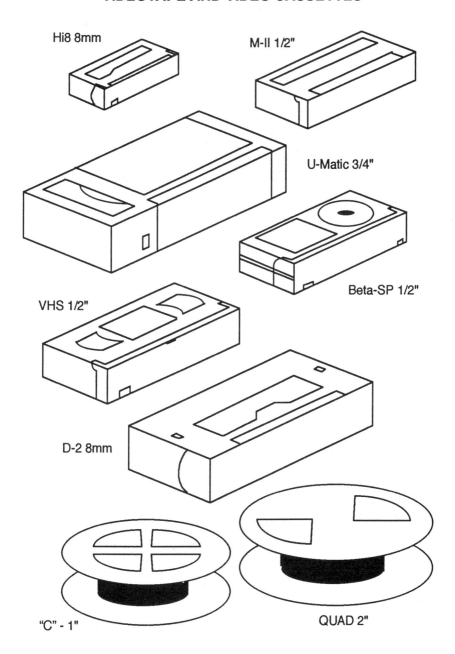

Hi8 8mm

M-II 1/2"

U-Matic 3/4"

Beta-SP 1/2"

VHS 1/2"

D-2 8mm

"C" - 1"

QUAD 2"

51

Videotape Recorder Operation

Today's video cassette recorder is relatively easy to operate because its controls parallel those of the universal audio cassette recorder. Once the cassette is inserted correctly into the machine and power is applied, either from batteries or from an AC power adapter source, operation is via the familiar functions of record, play, fast forward, rewind, and stop. On some tape decks there is an additional control marked "audio dub," which allows the audio level to be set before a recording is started. When pressed at the same time as the "play" control, it allows an audio recording to be made on audio track 1 without disturbing either the video track or audio track 2.

All tape decks contain some means of measuring the amount of tape that has been played or recorded. Consumer model recorders and lower priced professional recorders use a "tape counter" that counts the revolutions of the take-up reel. If the counter is set at zero when a new tape is loaded into the deck, it is possible to keep approximate track of where shots have been recorded on the cassette, thus enabling the operator or editor to find that same shot at a later time. But this counter is not linear; one revolution at the beginning of the reel may only contain a few seconds, while a revolution at the end of the reel may contain several minutes of recorded material. It is possible to chart approximately the amount of tape in each revolution by timing an entire cassette of tape.

Professional tape decks measure tape usage with an actual timer that indicates the amount of time in minutes and seconds that has elapsed from the moment the timer was zeroed. If the tape deck is equipped with a SMPTE time code source, it will indicate the location on the tape precisely to the hour, minute, second, and frame.

Most recorders include a multipurpose meter and a switch that can be set to read the video level, audio level, or state of the battery charge. A switch that allows manual or automatic gain control of the audio usually is located near this meter. Several warning lamps also may be a part of the control panel of the tape deck. These indicate when the machine is recording or is in pause, when the battery is running low, or when the tape stock is about to end. On more advanced machines there may be lamps that indicate high humidity, lack of servo lock, or other malfunctions of the machine.

Control Panels of Recorders

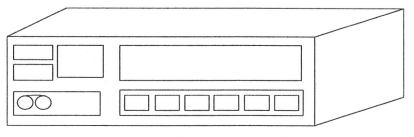

Consumer Recorder

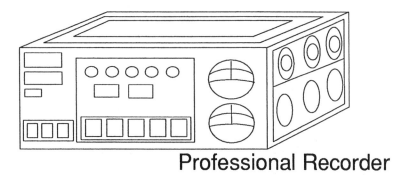

Professional Recorder

Connectors, Plugs, and Jacks I: Power and Audio

Before any discussion of connecting equipment together can be held, an understanding of the somewhat confusing world of cables and connectors must be reached. Unless a cable is permanently wired into a piece of equipment—such as a microphone, recorder, camera, monitor, or power source—the specific type of cable and specific cable connectors must be assembled and properly connected. The connector at either end of a cable is called a *plug;* the connector mounted on the wall or on the side of a piece of equipment is called a *jack.* There are both female and male plugs and jacks, and it takes one of each to make a connection. The contacts on a female plug are contained within the plug, the contacts project out of the male plug. There are three major types of plugs/jacks: power, audio, and video.

Power Connectors and Plugs
Power connectors are designed to carry either 110/220 volt AC, or 12 volt DC power. Connectors for AC power are the same as you will find on home appliances and mounted on the walls of homes and offices. Connectors for DC power may be either DIN (a German connector), a special XLR connector, or, for most VCRs, a special microplug used only for 12 v DC.

Audio Connectors and Plugs
Professional microphone audio connectors are called *XLRs* and have a clip on the female plug or jack that either locks the plug to the jack or locks two plugs together. The clip must be released in order to separate the plug from the jack. This type is the best audio connector to use because it cannot be unplugged accidentally and it contains three conductors in addition to a shield for the best audio transmission.

Many manufacturers use a mini-plug (sometimes called an *1/8-inch phone plug*) or an RCA plug (sometimes called a *phono plug*). Both of these connectors are used for microphone and high-level audio connectors and can be easily mistaken for each other. However, they are not compatible, and damage can occur if an RCA plug is forced into a mini-jack, or vice versa. Either of these plugs, mini or RCA, can be accidentally disconnected easily since they are held in place only by friction.

An older audio plug is the 1/4-inch (sometimes called *phone*) plug, probably because it was commonly used by the early telephone companies. Since it is easy to confuse the terms *phono* and *phone*, it is preferable to differentiate audio plugs by the alternate terms just listed.

AUDIO CONNECTORS

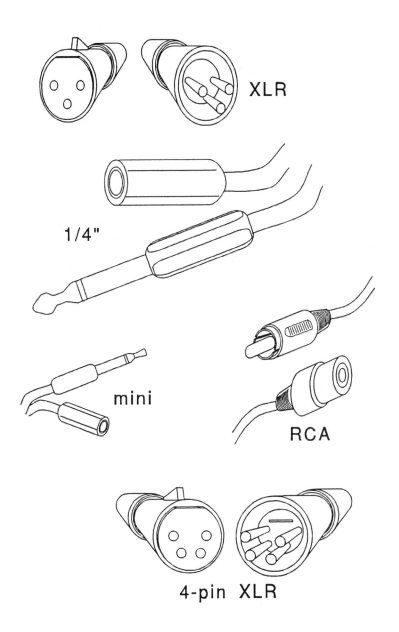

XLR

1/4"

mini

RCA

4-pin XLR

Connectors, Plugs and Jacks II: Video

There are four basic video plugs in common usage today. The RCA connector, unfortunately, has become standard for consumer video equipment. Because it is a friction plug, it can be unplugged unintentionally and easily, and it is a common audio connector, so cables may be misconnected by accident.

Professionals use a connector called a *BNC*, a name for which no two video specialists can agree upon its derivation. The most prevalent is "Bayonet Naval Connector," since it was first used by the Navy. It is designed so that it twist locks into place, making a sure connection, but is still easy to connect and/or disconnect with one hand.

An older video connector is called the *UHF connector*. It has a threaded collar that is tightened once the plug has been inserted into the jack. Because it is larger, more expensive, and more awkward to use, it appears on fewer new types of equipment.

BNC, RCA, and UHF connectors are all designed to carry only the video signal and are all male connectors. If cables need to be connected together, a female adapter called a *barrel* must be used between the cables.

There are two methods of transmitting both audio and video information through the same cable. The first uses separate conductors inside the cable for audio and video. The multi-pin camera and 8-pin monitor cables and plugs are examples of multiconductor cables. The second uses a special cable and connectors called *RF* or *F*. To use an RF cable, the audio and video signals must be combined into one signal using a circuit called a *modulator*. On the other end of the line, a *demodulator* must be present to separate the audio and video signals again. The RF connector is used by cable companies to connect their signal to a home receiver, and antennas are often connected with RF cables and plugs.

There are other cables and plugs used to carry video and audio signals, but the ones listed here are the most common.

VIDEO CONNECTORS

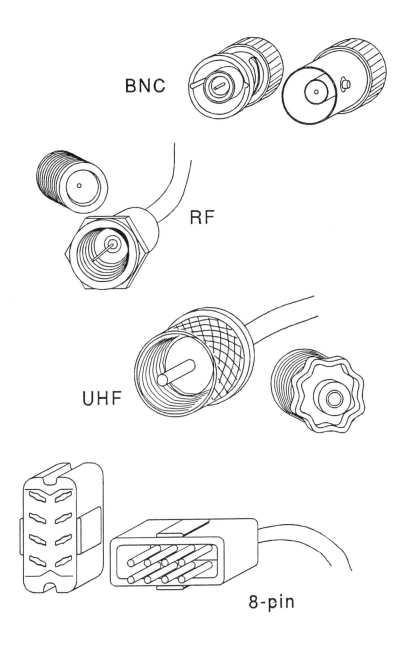

BNC

RF

UHF

8-pin

Connector Panel: Consumer Model Recorders

The operational portion of a video cassette recorder that contributes the most problems to the beginner is the connector panel. On a consumer model recorder it may contain only a multi-pin jack for the camera cable and either an AC power cord to plug into the wall or an internal battery pack.

Depending on the complexity and flexibility of the camera and the recorder combination, any or all of the following connectors and controls may be present.

Camera Cable Jack

The most obvious connector will be the camera cable jack, usually a 10- or 14-pin connector. The jack will have guide slots or pins that match the cable connector to make certain the pins and holes are properly aligned. To use, carefully align these guides, push in, and then turn the twist lock. Do not blindly insert the plug into the jack and twist until it mates. This method of alignment will tend to twist and bend the small pins, destroying the plug or the jack on the tape deck.

The camera cable carries video signals in both directions: from the camera to the deck and, for monitoring, from the deck back to the camera. It also carries all of the control signals between the camera and deck. Most cameras carry a built-in microphone, and that signal, as well as a headphone circuit, is carried in the camera cable. Camera power from the tape deck also is carried in the camera cable.

Power Connector

A 12 v DC connector, usually a micro-jack, may or may not be found on the connector panel. Often the 12 v jack will be located near the battery storage slot. Some decks, in addition to the micro power jack, may utilize either a 4-pin XLR or a 4-pin DIN jack for power sources.

Audio Jacks

Mounted on the panel also will be audio jacks, for both input and output. The input jacks will be either minis or XLR jacks. If the format has two audio channels, there will be an input jack for each channel. There also should be a switch to change the input level from mike to line level for each input jack. Audio outputs usually are RCA jacks, but in some cases also may be mini-jacks—once again, one for each channel.

On most tape decks an additional mini output jack for headphones is usually provided; often it is a stereo mini-jack so that both audio channels may be monitored simultaneously.

Consumer Deck
Connector Panel

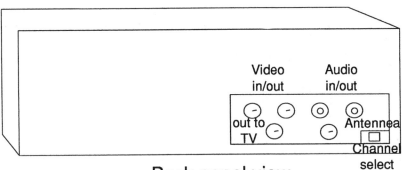

Video
in/out

Audio
in/out

out to
TV

Antennea

Channel
select

Back panel view

Connector Panel: Professional Model Recorders

Video Inputs and Outputs

All of the jacks normally located on consumer equipment also will be found on professional equipment. Additional connectors are indicated below. The video connectors on newer professional equipment are all BNC connectors. On older equipment, they may be UHF connectors, and on consumer equipment, RCA connectors are often found. All decks will have at least one video-input jack and one video-output jack. There may also be one additional jack for a sync signal, should more than one camera be used in a production, and another jack for a second video output.

If the camera cable or connectors fail for any reason, a video cable can be run directly from the camera to the tape deck. This will allow you to record video from the camera; audio and power lines will have to be run separately, and the control signals between the camera and deck, such as the remote recorder start/stop, will not be operable. In this situation, the camera will have to have its own batteries or other power source. Using a single video cable to connect the camera to the recorder allows the two to be much further apart when weather or other production situations require such a separation.

If there is a separate video input on the equipment, then a switch will be mounted next to it marked "line/camera" to make the choice between the camera cable or video connector inputs. On some decks there may be an RF connector. If the deck also contains within its circuits an RF modulator, then the combined audio and video signal is available at this jack. This signal may be viewed on a television receiver tuned to either channel 3 or 4 or fed directly into a consumer 1/2-inch deck.

Professional Deck
Connector Panel

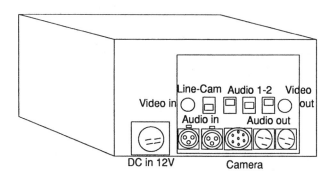

Side View

Connection Panel: Separate and Attached Units

Separate Camera and Recorder Units

If the production unit utilizes a camera and a separate recorder, then the two must be connected properly in order for each to function as they are intended. If the recorder and camera are designed to operate together, then a single multiconductor cable is sufficient. That one cable, generally with either a 10- or 14-pin connector, may carry power from the recorder to the camera and feed the video signal back to the monitor on the camera on playback from the recorder. The camera will feed a sync signal, the video signal, and the audio signal if the microphone is mounted or plugged into the camera.

If the recorder and camera are not matched, then an adapter cable may be needed to connect the two units. In some cases, some of the functions, such as remote start/stop, may not be operable if the camera and recorder are manufactured by different companies.

In most cases the microphone or other audio inputs are connected directly to the jack panel on the recorder.

Attached Camera and Recorder Units (Camcorders)

There are two types of camera/recorder (camcorder) attached units: single-piece and dockable. Single-piece units are manufactured so that the recorder and camera are one integrated unit constructed on a single frame with all connectors between the camera and recorder hard-wired internally. Dockable camcorders are designed so that the camera and recorder may be separated and even operated separately, if needed. The dockable unit allows for more flexibility in the choice of either unit. As an example, if a production did not require the highest quality of recording, the camera could be docked to a S-VHS or Hi8 recorder. The same camera also could be used on a high-quality production simply by switching to a dockable BetaSP recorder.

Both the dockable and single-piece units afford the convenience of avoiding broken or lost cables and/or connectors, becoming entangled in cables, and being limited by the length of the cable. The camcorder is also lighter than two separate units.

The disadvantage to a single unit during an electronic field production (EFP) is that the loading and adjusting of the recorder may disturb the position of the camera. It is also more difficult for a continuity assistant to read time code from the camera than from a separate recorder. Also, if either unit fails, then the whole unit must be taken out of service, rather than simply the unit that has failed.

Camera-Recorder Combinations

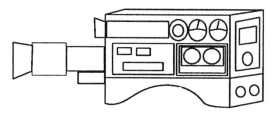

Camcorder-Dockable Unit

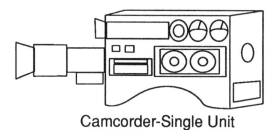

Camcorder-Single Unit

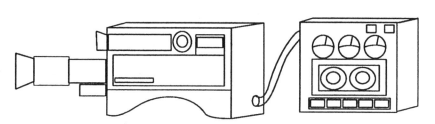

Separate Camera-Recorder Unit

Audio: Cables and Connectors

Audio in the past has been the forgotten half of the audio/video production world. With the arrival of digital audio, and increased audience awareness of the value of quality sound, audio production now has become much more important than in years past.

Two developments in audio have contributed to the ability of production personnel to improve the quality of their audio: digital audio and the condenser microphone. Both have reduced the size of audio equipment and measurably increased its sensitivity and frequency response.

Cables and Connectors

As with video cables and connectors, there is no universal standard for audio connectors. Some differences exist due to the origins of the equipment, others to level of production professionalism, and still others to the physical size of the equipment.

At the professional level, all microphone-level audio connectors are XLR, three-contact-plus-shield, balanced-line cables and connectors. The signal is carried on the two internal wires, with the third connected to the shield. This system provides the maximum protection against outside audio interference and noise. Some professional equipment utilizes RCA (phono) plugs for line-level input and output audio connectors. This implies that the cable would be a single conductor with shield and designed to operate with an unbalanced circuit. With line-level signals, the higher signal is less affected by outside signals. Some other audio circuits, such as headphones, may use a miniplug as a connector.

Prosumer, a production level requiring equipment above consumer, but below that of professional, and consumer equipment may dispense with balanced lines and XLR connectors, using only RCA and miniplugs for all audio circuits. The advantage of RCA and miniplugs is their small size and low cost. However, their disadvantages—becoming easily unplugged and making poor electrical contact—far outweigh their advantages for a professional. An unbalanced line may pick up FM signals from close-by radio transmitters and noise generated by any equipment operating in either the audio or radio frequency (RF) ranges. An unbalanced mike line should be no longer than 5 to 10 feet to minimize picking up such noise and interfering signals.

BALANCED vs. UNBALANCED LINES & CONNECTORS

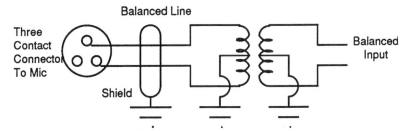

Balanced line and 3-contact connector (XLR)
Two internal shielded lines and
grounded shield

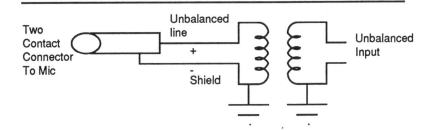

Unbalanced line and 2-contact connector (RCA-Phono, Mini, Phone)
One internal shielded line and
grounded shield.
[May act as an antenna and pick up radio signals]

Microphone Types

Microphones are categorized in three ways: by their element construction, pickup pattern, and electronic type. In addition, microphone choices are also made on the basis of their specific purpose or the type of audio pickup required.

Electronic Types

Microphone types are either *low impedance* or *high impedance.* Impedance is a complex measurement of resistance which also includes inductance and capacitance. All professional mikes are low-impedence. A low-impedence mike ideally should be connected to a two-conductor-plus-shield cable and XLR connector. This allows for connection to a balanced circuit, which provides the best audio pickup. High-impedance mikes are connected to a single-conductor cable and either an RCA or miniplug and should not be used more than 5 to 10 feet away from an amplifier.

Some consumer microphones are low impedance but are connected to the recorder with a single-conductor, unbalanced line, which is a compromise between professional low-impedance and consumer high-impedance circuit connection.

Element Types

Microphone element (transducer) types today are *dynamic* (moving coil), *ribbon,* or *condenser.* The dynamic mike is the most common, most rugged, and, for fast-moving coverage such as news or documentaries, provides the best frequency response for the least cost. The pickup coil converts soundwave energy to electric energy without an outside power source or amplification. These mikes can be designed to be relatively small and in any pickup pattern.

The ribbon mike is intended for studio or booth use only since it is heavy, large, and very sensitive to movement, shock, or wind. It does create a fine vocal quality, especially for the male voice. Its transducing element is a thin corrugated ribbon suspended between the two poles of a heavy magnet. A ribbon mike could be used on EFP shoots if the environment were controlled and it is kept out of inclement weather.

The condenser microphone is gradually replacing most other mikes. Originally it was expensive, heavy, large, and required amplifiers and power supplies located adjacent to the mike. With solid-state circuits and minipreamplifiers powered by small batteries or by current supplied from the amplifier (phantom power), the condenser mike has become much more practical. With its built-in preamplifier, it is very sensitive, has a fine frequency response, and is small and lightweight. The condenser mike can be designed in any pickup pattern and is manufactured in a variety of forms and price ranges.

66

MICROPHONE ELEMENTS

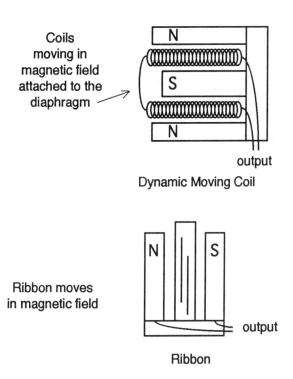

Coils moving in magnetic field attached to the diaphragm

output

Dynamic Moving Coil

Ribbon moves in magnetic field

output

Ribbon

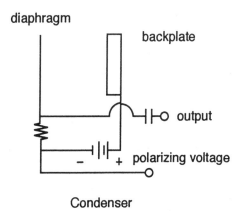

diaphragm

backplate

output

polarizing voltage

Condenser

Microphone Pickup Patterns

There are three basic pickup patterns: omnidirectional, unidirection, and bidirectional. Bidirectional mikes have little use in field productions and are best reserved for studio productions. If the shoot is staged in a controlled environment or interior location, a bidirectional mike may be used for interviews. Its name is derived from its ability to pick up sound from two sides equally while suppressing sound from the other two sides.

Omnidirectional mikes pick up sound from all directions, 360 degrees around the mike, with nearly equal sensitivity in all directions. All EFP audio kits should contain at least one good omnidirectional mike for crowd pickup and ambient noise recording.

The general background ambient noise of a location is called either *wild sound* or *nat* (short for "natural") *sound*. Wild or nat sound is very useful material to record for use in editing to provide an audio transition between scenes and to create the atmosphere of the original location for later voice-over narration.

The most useful mikes are those that are derived from the unidirectional mike. A true unidirectional mike will pick up sound only from the end of the mike. An extreme example of a unidirectional mike is a *shotgun mike*. It is designed to have a very narrow, (as narrow as 5 degrees) pickup pattern. Its sensitive area is predominately straight out from the mike, but there are nodes or areas to the side and behind within which sound also may be picked up. This cannot be avoided, even with the best and most expensive shotgun mikes. The audio kit of any EFP operator should contain several shotgun mikes of various lengths and pickup patterns.

The cardioid mike is a special type of unidirectional mike designed to combine the pickup pattern of the uni- and omnidirectional mikes to create a heart-shaped pattern in front of the mike. This provides the ideal pattern for an interviewer to hand-hold a mike between two people, to use the mike while describing an event without picking up too much background noise, and as a close-miked shotgun. If only a single mike may be carried, then a cardioid is the best choice.

Some professional microphones are designed with variable directional settings; that is, they may be adjusted with a switch on the case to be omnidirectional, unidirectional, or cardioid. As with all equipment, multi-purpose electronic equipment seldom performs as satisfactorily as equipment designed to perform a specific function.

Microphone Pickup Patterns

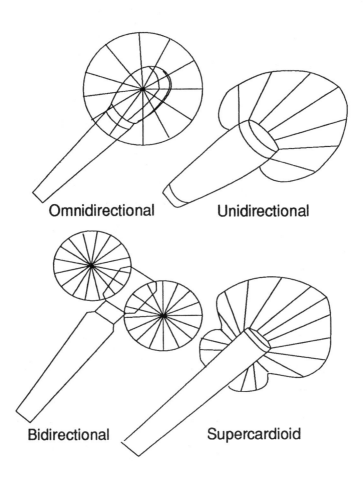

Omnidirectional

Unidirectional

Bidirectional

Supercardioid

Microphone Mounting

Microphones may be mounted at the end of a small hand-held boom called a *fishpole* or on a small, movable tripod-mounted boom called a *giraffe*, or, if space allows, on a large wheeled boom that the operator rides called a *perambulator*. The type of mike usually mounted on booms is a cardioid or short shotgun. The mike could be hung from a gaffer hook from the ceiling; from a hanging light fixture, door, or window frame; or from any other stable piece of tall furniture in the room. A third method of mike placement is to hide it behind objects between the talent and the camera: floral arrangements on a table, books, telephones, or any other set piece large enough to hide the mike and its stand. Another method is to place a unidirectional mike on the body of the subject. The mike may be attached in plain view, hanging from the neck as a lavalier, or a smaller peanut mike may be attached under the talent's necktie, shirt, or blouse or to a jacket lapel.

The mike may be wired directly to the recorder, or it may be a wireless mike feeding a small transmitter hidden on the body of the talent and picked up by a small receiver wired to the recorder. Wireless mikes are becoming more popular as the price and their sensitivity to other RF signals in the area are reduced. The earliest wireless mikes picked up taxi-cab and police radio signals, making them unusable for some applications. Today's transmitters are designed to be smaller and more powerful, correcting many of the past problems.

Each individual production requirement will determine the best mike for that situation. Follow general recommendations listed in this section, other books and articles on microphone usage and placement, and finally, remember that experience and experimentation are the best teachers.

For some field productions—such as sporting events, game shows, and live coverage of nonvideo events—the microphone need not be hidden. Those situations allow you to place the mike or mikes in the best position for maximum quality and/or sensitivity of audio pickup. The mike should be placed in direct line with the performer's mouth, below the face, and depending on type of microphone, approximately 12 to 15 inches from the mouth. The microphone should be close enough for clear pickup and the exclusion of unwanted sounds, but far enough away to avoid picking up the popping of "Ps" and other plosive sounds.

Also the mike should be placed so that its pickup will match the approximate perspective of the picture; that is, if it is an extreme wide shot, then the audio should sound off-mike, and if it is a tight close-up, then the pickup should be very intimate and close-miked.

Often the type of environment—closed-in small room, out in the open, or a large, echo-filled auditorium—partially determines the best choice of microphone.

70

MICROPHONE MOUNTING DEVICES

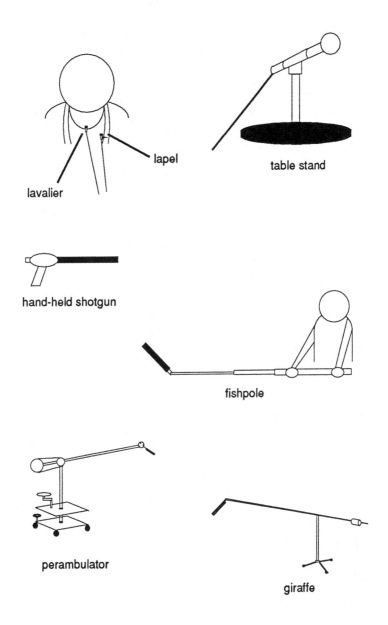

lapel

lavalier

table stand

hand-held shotgun

fishpole

perambulator

giraffe

Audio Recording Considerations

Non-miked Audio Sources

In addition to recording audio from microphones, you may find it necessary to record nonmiked audio sources. Such sources may be the output of amplifiers, public address systems, or tape or disc decks. Each of these are high-level outputs and need to be fed into a high-level, high-impedance input on the recorder. Matching impedance and level is critical for a satisfactory recording. Check the output specifications of the high-level source and match it to the specifications of the recorder being used. If they do not match, then a matching transformer or amplifier should be inserted into the circuit to guarantee a proper match.

Which Audio Track to Use

Another audio consideration is the choice of audio channel to record on the videotape. All professional videotape machines offer more than one track for audio recording. The U-matic has two: Channel 1 is located on the edge of the tape, and channel 2 is located just inside channel 1. Channel 2 is the better track to use because channel 1 can become stretched or wrinkled. Betacam and M-II also have two longitudinal tracks, except channel 2 is on the outside and channel 1 is on the inside. One-inch "C" format has three audio tracks. Number 1 is on the inside and numbers 2 and 3 are on the opposite outside positions.

Advanced videotape formats—such as S-VHS, Hi8, BetaSP, and M-II—also have audio tracks recorded digitally within the video signal. These tracks are usually stereo and are very high quality, but they are difficult to edit because they are part of, and cannot be separated from, the video signal. However, they can be edited and dubbed to a longitudinal track on another tape (losing some of the quality in the process).

Audio pickup often is ignored or thought of as a last item when in reality audio often carries more than half the critical information in a story. It is important, then, to plan seriously for and spend time properly setting up microphones, mixers, and cables and choosing audio channels for the best possible audio recording along with the video recording.

AUDIO TRACK LOCATIONS ON VIDEOTAPE FORMATS

1/2" CONSUMER

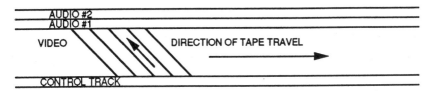

3/4" U-MATIC

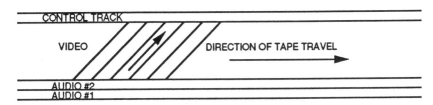

1/2" PROFESSIONAL

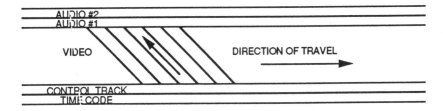

1" TYPE "C"

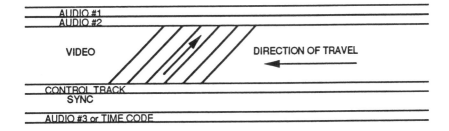

Lighting Instruments

The function of lighting at its simplest is to provide enough illumination so that the camera can reproduce an image. The complexity of lighting and lighting techniques is drawn from the need for the instruments to serve the aesthetic needs of the medium: to set mood, time, and location and to draw attention to the critical portions of the frame.

Lighting instruments have evolved from both the stage and motion-picture industries, just as most audio equipment evolved from the radio and motion-picture industries.

Floodlights

There are three basic types of field lighting instruments: floodlights, focusing spotlights, and fixed-focus instruments. *Floodlights* provide a broad relatively uncontrolled, soft diffused light that is used to cover large areas and to fill in shadow areas. The most common field floods are softlights, broads, and umbrella lights. Softlights are the largest, but because they are now constructed of folding aluminum frames and cloth reflector covers, they are portable.

Broads are smaller, box-like instruments usually equipped with some type of barndoor to control the coverage of light. They most commonly contain one lamp.

Umbrella lighting is more of a technique than a specific type of instrument since any spotlight can be fitted with an umbrella. The concept is simply to focus the light from a spotlight onto an umbrella shaped reflector mounted on the instrument so that the light strikes the inner concave surface of the umbrella and is reflected back in the opposite direction.

Focusing Spotlights

Focusing spotlights are either open faced without a lens or lensed with a Fresnel or plano-convex lens. Focusing spots are essential for critical creative lighting.

Fixed-Focus Instruments

Fixed-focus instruments are designed around a lamp similar to an auto headlight. A bank of these lamps is built into a cabinet that allows each lamp to be turned on and aimed individually. Their main purpose is to light a wide area with an even but controlled field of light. The lamps are called *FAY* if the output is 5400° Kelvin (K), and *PAR* if the output is 3,200° K (see Color Temperature).

All of the above instruments are designed to operate from portable floor stands and be powered by 110 or 220 v AC power. They also can be mounted from a variety of gaffer mounts on walls, doors, or other sturdy objects.

LIGHTING INSTRUMENTS

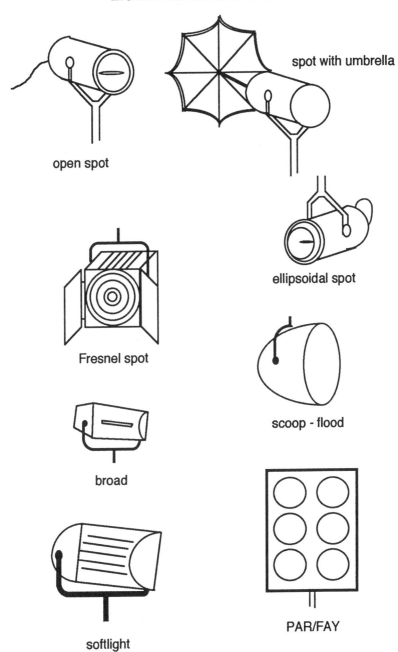

open spot

spot with umbrella

ellipsoidal spot

Fresnel spot

scoop - flood

broad

softlight

PAR/FAY

75

Controlling and Powering Light

Controlling Light

Because field production seldom allows for the use of a portable light dimmer board, control over the light output becomes critical for creative shooting situations. Two simple, portable techniques are used: reflectors and tents. *Reflectors* are large foam boards covered on one side with a variety of surfaces; plain white, colored, or textured. These reflectors are used to throw a soft fill light into areas not easily reached with instruments or to provide light when an instrument is not available or would cast an additional shadow.

Tents diffuse light, allowing the use of a number of instruments without creating unwanted shadows.

An EFP lighting kit should contain a set of gaffer's accessories: gobos, clamps, stands, weights, brackets, reflectors, and gaffer tools. A gaffer is a lighting technician. Some of the equipment used by a gaffer are pieces of fabric used to block light called gobos and electrician tools such as wrenches and pliers.

Power Sources

For field production there are three sources of power: the alternating current present in most buildings, batteries, and portable generators.

Portable generators are expensive, noisy, and, for video cameras, an uncertain source of stable power. The instability presents no problem for lighting directors, but the noise and expense might present problems for the producer and/or the director. Batteries, except for ENG crews, are not dependable or powerful enough for most EFP production situations. ENG is the abbreviation for electronic news gathering, a specialized form of single-camera video production. ENG crews work in a variety of locations where electrical power is readily not available and therefore must rely on batteries.

The most dependable source of power for lighting is the AC circuits in most buildings. Since lighting instruments draw much more current than any other piece of equipment, some knowledge of wattage, current, and voltage is necessary. The standard power in this country is delivered between 110 and 120 v. The lamps in lighting instruments are rated in watts, and the rating on power circuits in buildings is in amperage (amps). You can perform the simple translation of watts to amps or vice versa by using Ohms Law: Wattage equals Voltage times Amperage. If voltage is treated as a constant of 100 (this provides a built-in 10 percent safety margin), then to find wattage, simply multiple amps times 100. To find amps from known wattage, simply divide wattage by 100. Both can be done easily without a calculator.

APPLICATION OF OHM'S LAW TO TYPICAL LIGHTING SET-UP

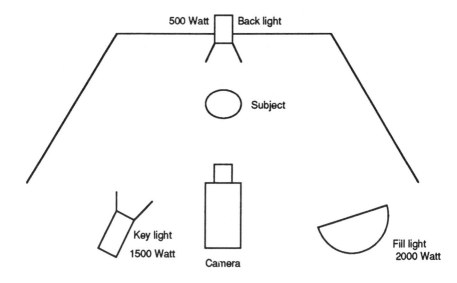

Ohm's Law : Wattage = Voltage x Amperage

$$W = V \times A$$

Assume V = 100 V as a constant

To find Amperage : $A = \dfrac{W}{100}$

To find Wattage: W = A x 100

In the example above: Back light = 500 W

Key light = 1500 W

Fill light = <u>2000 W</u>

TOTAL = 4000 W

Amperage = $\dfrac{\underline{Wattage}}{100}$

Amperage = $\dfrac{\underline{4000}}{100}$

Amperage = 40 A

77

Color Temperature

The final consideration in lighting equipment actually is a part of the camera operation, but the problem starts with the source of light. All light sources are not equal in their actual color. The human eye and mind compensate for this variation by creating the illusion that light within a certain range appears white. Actual measurement of the color of light is in degrees Kelvin based on the color of a carbon heated and measured at certain temperatures. The lower the Kelvin temperature, the more reddish yellow the color of the light. The higher the Kelvin temperature, the bluer the light.

There is no actual "white" light on the Kelvin scale. Typical candlelight would measure below 1,800° K; an ordinary incandescent light bulb, 2,800° K; professional tungsten-halogen lamps, 3,200° K; daylight varies from approximately 4,000° K to over 12,000° K, but the standard is considered 5,400° K. The lower the Kelvin temperature, the "warmer" the color; the higher the Kelvin temperature, the "cooler" the color.

The critical factor concerning the color temperature is that a camera sees and reproduces the actual color of the light source as it is reflected from the subjects. An electronic camera can be adjusted to compensate for any variation in the color temperature by the process of white balancing. In order to properly light a scene, though, it should be lit with consistently color-balanced light sources.

Professional lamps are accurately rated for their color output, but when shooting in the field, you may be in an environment where the light sources are not controlled. Home incandescent lighting is warmer than studio lighting; office fluorescent lighting is bluer and greener (fluorescent lamps do not have a specific Kelvin temperature since they are a pulse light); and if shooting next to a window, the daylight entering will not match the color temperature of the production lamps. This situation is called *mixed lighting*.

It is necessary when lighting to take into consideration the color temperature of the available light sources by measuring them with a Kelvin temperature meter or by arranging to have all light sources be of the same color temperature.

COLOR TEMPERATURE OF LIGHT SOURCES

Color Temperature	Light Sources
1,850° K	Open flame
2,000° K	Worn household lamp Sunrise, sunset
2,800° K	Unshaded new household lamp
3,200° K	Quartz-Halogen studio lamp
3,400° K	Photoflood lamp
4,250° K	Early morning, late afternoon sunlight
4,800° K*	Fluorescent lamp
5,000° K	Carbon arc lamp
5,400° K	Noon sunlight
5,600° K	HMI lamp
6,000° K	Overcast sunlight
8,000-20,000° K	Direct blue sunlight

* Fluorescent lamps are pulse lamps and do not emit a specific color temperature, but do emit light with a high blue-green content that may be compensated for with proper filtering.

Measuring Light Intensity

In addition to measuring the Kelvin temperature of the light sources for the best lighting, it is necessary to measure the intensity of the light sources and the light reflected from the subjects.

The measurement of the light from the light sources (*incident light*) is accomplished by pointing an incident light meter at the light source. The measurement of the light from the subject (*reflected light*) is accomplished with a reflected light meter pointed at specific areas of the subject.

Some light meters are designed to permit both types of meter readings, but professional-quality meters are designed specifically to read either reflected or incident light levels. The two methods of taking light level readings are required in order to determine the two types of lighting ratios necessary for quality lighting.

Lighting Ratio
Regardless of the cost of a video camera, some minimum amount of light is required to produce an acceptable picture, called *base light*. An incident light reading of the amount of light falling on the subject gives the lighting director two pieces of information: the base light level necessary to produce an acceptable picture and the ratio of fill light to key light. By pointing the meter from the subject toward the lights with just the fill light turned on and then taking another reading with fill and key lights on, a numerical ratio is determined, called the *lighting ratio*. The standard starting lighting ratio is 2:1; that is, twice as much light from the key and fill as from the fill alone. A back light ratio may also be taken and it should be close to 1:1; that is, the back light should approximately equal the key light.

Contrast Ratio
The measurement for *contrast ratio* is a little more complex. A reflected spotlight meter is needed to measure accurately the amount of light reflected from the brightest object in the picture and the light reflected from the darkest object. The difficult part is that when there are either highly reflective or very dark objects in the frame, it is not necessary to include these areas in the readings if it is not necessary to be able to reproduce detail in either of those areas.

If the amount of light reflected from the brightest portion of the frame in which detail is necessary reflects more than 30 times more light than the darkest areas needed for detail, then more fill light will be needed on the dark areas or some light will have to be taken off the lightest areas.

Carefully lighting for the contrast range of the video camera will avoid having areas "blooming" or "flaring" into a white mass, or important areas appearing so dark that they look "muddy."

80

Basic Three-Point Lighting Plot
With Measurement Positions

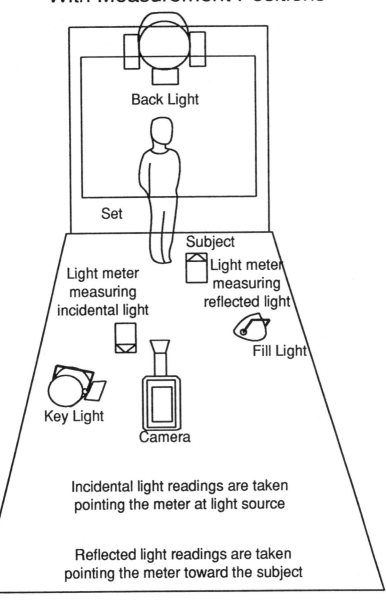

Back Light

Set

Subject

Light meter measuring incidental light

Light meter measuring reflected light

Fill Light

Key Light

Camera

Incidental light readings are taken
pointing the meter at light source

Reflected light readings are taken
pointing the meter toward the subject

Preproduction Planning I

Before any serious work may begin on a video project, a source of funding must be found. Money for staff, crew, cast, research, facilities, equipment, and expendable materials must be located and committed by an interested party. Such sources of funds may be clients who have contracted for the specific project, such as television stations or networks, cable networks, or funding agencies: government agencies, money-lending agencies, such as banks, savings and loan companies, or insurance companies.

Proposal

Regardless of the funding source, there is common information that must be supplied in order to gain access to such funding. The first document of the preproduction process is called a *proposal*. A proposal generally is the responsibility of the producer but is better written with the assistance of the writer(s) and director. Considerable knowledge of the subject is imperative to avoid mistakes, misinformation, or serious inaccuracy. A complete site survey, interviews, and library and other research must be carried out before the proposal can be written.

Once research has been completed, all of the information is organized into a concise, meaningful package that briefly explains the objective of the production, the goals, target audience, and distribution methods. Key production factors, basic style and genre, unusual production techniques, and special casting and location considerations—along with the length, recording and release formats—all need to be explained in easy-to-understand lay terms. It is important that the proposal writer understand that a nonmedia person may be reading the proposal, and reaching a funding judgment. It must be written so that all aspects of the production are presented clearly, avoiding production jargon.

An approximate time line and budget complete the proposal package. Both of these should be prepared carefully and realistically. Too much or too little of either can discourage a client or funding source. Worse yet, either miscalculation can place the producer in a position where it is impossible to complete the project because of insufficient funds or time.

SAMPLE PROPOSAL FORMAT

Rivers and Streams Productions, Inc. will produce a ten minute, color videotape to be used as a training medium for new and present employees of Mountain Industries. The tape will target specific safety procedures necessary to follow in the unique operation of logging in the mountains of Montana. The tape will emphasize personal safety actions and procedures required by the Occupational Safety and Health Administration.

The shooting schedule will last for ten days, weather and other acts of nature not withstanding. Postproduction will last for four weeks following the completion of principle videography. Taping will start within two weeks of final script approval.   Research and preparing of the treatment will last three weeks following the acceptance of the proposal. The final script will be prepared within three weeks of acceptance of the proposed treatment.

The budget will be approximately $35,000.00, depending on specific technical requirements of the script. Because the script calls for a series of dangerous actions requiring stunt actors and technicians, some allowances for costs and shooting overruns may be required.

The format will be semi-documentary/instructional with the tape narrated and techniques explained by an actor representing a skilled and knowledgeable logger. Both incorrect and correct operational procures will be illustrated. Employees, equipment, and facilities of Mountain Industries logging operation will be required for the production of this tape.

Preproduction Planning II

Treatment

Once the proposal has been written, a treatment is then prepared. A *treatment* is a narrative description of the production. Like the proposal, the treatment is intended to be read by the potential funding source to assist in making a decision as to whether they are willing to trust their money to the producer.

The preliminary paragraph of the treatment repeats key information from the proposal: title, length, format, and objective of the production. It is assumed the proposal and treatment will be presented and read at the same time.

The treatment should be written as if the writer were describing what he or she sees when watching a playback of the completed production. Dialogue is not used, but indications of the type of conversations or narration should be included. Also, professional terminology such as "dissolve," "medium close-up," and "voice-over" are to be avoided. Remember, the person reading the document is not a media professional. It is imperative that any person who controls money be able to make sense of the proposal and the treatment, which are, in essence, sales tools designed to sell your ability to successfully complete your production within budget and on time, while accomplishing the stated objective.

Your potential funding source should be able to read these two documents and easily be able to imagine exactly what the production will sound and look like without any other explanation or verbal description on the part of the producer.

In reality, both the proposal and treatment may be written *after* the script has been finalized, since the proposal and treatment must accurately reflect the script. From a practical point of view, the three preproduction writing functions may be composed simultaneously.

Scene script

The first completed draft of a script is called a *scene script*. It contains a detailed description of each scene and the action occurring during that scene, but not specific shots. Each scene should indicate whether it is set during the day or at night and in an interior or exterior setting, the characters, and key furniture or objects present, character movements, and all dialogue and narration.

Shooting Script

The *shooting script* is a more detailed version of the scene script. Each shot is described specifically and numbered in order. The framing—WS, MCU, CU—is indicated, but the writer leaves some leeway for the director's creativity. The descriptions should be complete enough so that the director is able to interpret accurately what the writer had intended in each sequence, scene, or shot.

SAMPLE TREATMENT FORMAT

TITLE: Safety Training   PAGE: 1
WRITER: T. Bartlett   LENGTH: 10 mins
CLIENT: Mountain Industries   DATE: 10-10-92

The ten-minute training tape will open with a montage of incorrect logging operations followed in each case by the possible disastrous and life-threatening results of such actions. Examples of such scenes are:

A logger without a safety belt stepping back and falling from tree stand.

A chainsaw jamming and flipping back into the logger.

A tractor tipping over on the driver because it exceeded its tilt limit.

A logging truck driven too fast forces an on-coming car from the road.

A logger struck by a log falling from a truck being loaded because he was standing too close to the truck.

A fire caused by a logger refueling his saw improperly.

A run-away truck or tractor left improperly locked down.

A logger dumped into the river and crushed by logs.

A log avalanche caused by careless blocking of a log stack.

This series of accidents will be enhanced with sound effects and dramatic music as well as the actual sound of each accident.

Following this montage, the narrator will walk into the scene and describe in general the dangers and reasons for following OSHA safety requirements for those working in dangerous occupations such as the

(continued)

Single-Column Script Format

There are two basic script formats used in preparing scripts for EFP, the traditional film single-column format and the traditional television dual-column format.

The *single-column format* evolved from stage script format to motion-picture format to radio before it was adapted again for video productions. The format indicates various aspects of the scripts by varying the width of the margins and by capitalizing certain portions of the copy. The rules at first seem complex, but can be summarized as follows:

- Each shot starts with the shot number at the extremes of the right- and left-hand margins. In uppercase type, either the word *DAY* or *NIGHT* indicates lighting conditions, followed by either *INT* or *EXT*, to indicate location.
- Camera directions, scene descriptions, and stage directions are typed next, within slightly narrower margins. How the line is to be delivered is typed in still narrower margins within parentheses, and dialogue is typed within even narrower margins.
- The name of the speaking character is centered above his or her line in upper-case letters.
- Single-spacing is used for dialogue, camera angles and movements, stage directions, scene descriptions, sound effects, or cues.
- Double-spacing is used to separate a camera shot or scene from the next camera shot or scene, a scene from an interceding transition (FADE IN/FADE OUT, DISSOLVE), the speech of one character from the heading of the next character, and a speech from camera or stage directions.
- Upper-case type is used for: INT or EXT in heading line; indication of location; indication of day/night; name of a character when first introduced in the stage directions and to indicate their dialogue; camera angles and movements; scene transitions; and (CONTINUED), if a scene is split between pages (avoid if at all possible).

SINGLE COLUMN SCRIPT FORMAT

(Margins and tabs set as indicated below. assuming 80 space wide paper)

| 5 | 10 | 20 | 25 | 55 | 60 | 70 | 75 |

FADE IN:

1.   INT./EXT.   DAY/NIGHT   1.
       BRIEF SCENE OR SHOT DESCRIPTION, CAM. ANGLE.

In upper and lower case, a more detailed description of the scene giving setting, props, and CHARACTERS position if needed with margins set at 10/70.

> CHARACTER
> (Mode of delivery, upper and
> lower case, margins at 25/55)

> The dialog is typed in upper and lower case
> centered within 20/60 margins.

Any other descriptions of shot framing, movement of CAMERA or CHARACTER is at margins set at 10/70.

                                         (TRANSITION)

2.   INT   WS   UNIVERSITY CLASSROOM   DAY   2.

Classroom is full of students, some wide awake, gossiping, others sleeping or nodding off as they wait for the professor to arrive.

> JANE
> (Quietly so only Jack can hear her.)
> Are you sure there isn't going to be an exam
> during tomorrow's class?

> JACK
> (With a bravado, all-knowing tone)
> Of course not, have I ever lied to you?

The professor enters the room, downstage right, walks to the lecturn and the room becomes quiet.

> PROFESSOR
> (Emphatically as a reminder)
> If I am forced to repeat myself again, I WILL
> be forced to give you your first examination in
> tomorrow's class.

                                  (DISSOLVE TO)

3.   EXT   WS   CAMPUS   DAY   3.

The clouds suddenly darken the sky as rain, thunder and lightning start and the lights go out plunging the room into darkness.

(A scene script describes the entire scene in very general terms, a shooting script contains much more detailed descriptions and shot instructions)

Dual-Column Script Format

Dual-column television script *format* evolved from audio-visual format and instructional film format. This format is based on separating audio instructions and information from visual instructions. Two columns are set up on the page. Today the video is located on the left side of the page, the audio on the right. This is not an absolute rule; some operations prefer the opposite, and some include a storyboard on the left, right, or down the middle of the page.

Each shot number is indicated in both the video and audio columns, matching the appropriate audio with its video. All video instructions are typed in upper-case letters, as are all audio instructions. Copy to be read by the performers is typed in upper- and lower-case letters. Many performers, especially news anchors, prefer all upper-case letters in the misguided belief that upper-case copy is easier to read. However, all readability studies indicate the opposite, and today most computerized prompter systems display copy in upper- and lower-case letters.

Video instructions are arranged in single-spaced blocks; audio copy, in double-spaced blocks. Triple-spacing between shots helps both the talent and the director follow the flow of the script. The name of the talent is typed in upper-case letters to the left of the right-hand column. If the same audio source continues through several shots, it is not necessary to repeat the source's name unless another source intervenes.

Avoid hyphenating words at the end of a line and avoid splitting shots at the bottom of the page. Spreading copy out allows for notes and additional instructions to be added during actual production.

Information concerning the production should be repeated at the top of each page: title, writer's name and other pertinent information. Each page must be numbered in sequence. If pages are added, letters or other indications may be added to keep the pages in order (for example, page 25a falls between pages 25 and 26).

DUAL COLUMN SCRIPT FORMAT

TITLE: PAGE:
WRITER: LENGTH:
CLIENT: DATE:

VIDEO	AUDIO
1. SINGLE SPACE VIDEO INSTRUCTIONS	1. ANNCR: Audio copy is lined up directly across the page from its matching video.
2. TRIPLE SPACE BETWEEN EACH SHOT	2. Double space between each line of audio copy.
3. EACH SHOT MUST BE NUMBERED ON THE SCRIPT	3. The audio column's number must match that of its video.
4. EVERYTHING THE VIEWER IS TO SEE; ALL VISUALS, VIDEO TAPES, CG, CAMERA SHOTS, ARE INCLUDED IN THE LEFT-HAND COLUMN.	4. Everything the viewer is to hear; all sounds, music, voices, sound effects, narration and all audio cues are included in the right-hand column.
5. EVERYTHING ON THE VIDEO SIDE IS TYPED IN CAPITOL LETTERS.	5. Everything spoken by the talent is typed in upper and lower case letters. All instructions in the audio column are typed in capitol letters.
6. THE TALENT'S NAME STARTS EACH NEW LINE, BUT DOES NOT HAVE TO BE REPEATED IF THE SAME PERSON OR SOUND SOURCE CONTINUES.	6. SAM: Note--the name is in caps, what Sam says is in upper and lower case.
7. AVOID SPLITTING SHOTS AT BOTTOM OF THE PAGE.	7. Avoid splitting words or thoughts at the end of the line.

91

Storyboards

Storyboards are paper visualizations of the production. They provide a flexible means of working out sequences, framing, and shot relationships before bringing an expensive cast and crew together for the actual production. Storyboards are usually organized in three parts: picture, copy/instructions, and shot number.

Generally a storyboard form displays a 3:4 area with rounded corners that contains the video frame, with a small space above the frame for writing in the shot number. Below the frame is an area, usually slightly smaller than the frame, designed to contain the audio and/or other specific instructions for that shot.

The key objects in the shot are sketched into the frame block. These visual representations can be as simple as stick figures or as accurate as color photographs. The more accurate the drawings, the more serviceable the storyboard will be in solving probems during preproduction and production. The matching space for instructions may contain "pan," "dolly," or other camera movement or composition concepts. The shot number must match the shot number on the script. If additions or deletions are made, then the shot-number changes must be made to both script and storyboard. Each shot should be represented by at least one storyboard frame. In some cases, additional frames may be necessary to show beginning and ending frame positions if a pan, dolly, or zoom is indicated.

Once completed, storyboard frames can be placed on a wall or flannel board so they can be rearranged easily. Standing back and looking at all of the storyboard frames gives the director, writer, and producer a better overall view of the production and can provide the means to spot problem areas or solutions to problems.

Since the storyboard frame, description, and shot number can be separated from other storyboard frames, they can be manipulated until the best possible shot sequence is reached. This process may prevent continuity problems by avoiding jump cuts and may create a more organized method of shooting the production.

Once the complete storyboard order has been arranged, then the final shooting script can be written.

Story Boards

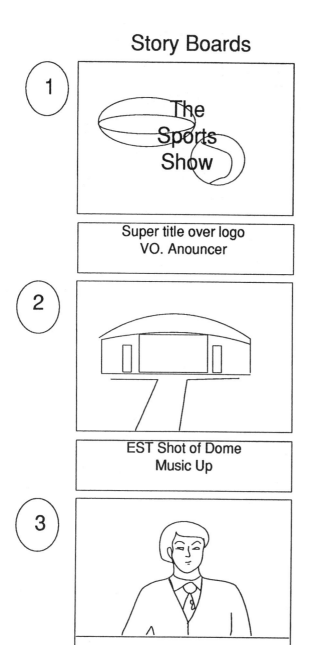

1

The
Sports
Show

Super title over logo
VO. Anouncer

2

EST Shot of Dome
Music Up

3

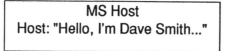

MS Host
Host: "Hello, I'm Dave Smith..."

Location Scouting

A general notion of the type of shooting location required should have been determined early on in the production conceptualization process. Specific locations can be chosen after the scene script has been written, but the location must be finalized before the shooting script has been completed.

Besides the obvious characteristics to look for in a location—accessibility and having the right setting or appearance—are some that are less than obvious. A cost-free location near parking, power, and sanitary facilities and convenient to storage space for equipment and materials is worth searching for. Also valuable would be temperature-controlled areas for cast and crew to use between takes. Once a location has been decided upon, a meeting with the site authority must be arranged.

At this meeting, the following information must be collected: names, phone numbers, and exact location or addresses of authorities who control the areas and locations to be used. This person may be the resident, building engineer, building manager, janitor, department head, or a civil employee in charge of public areas. Make certain the person who has given permission to use the location actually has the authority to do so and then get it in writing with a location release.

While meeting with the site authority, the producer should explain fully how the site is to be used, what changes may be necessary, how restoration will be handled, and what access the production crew will have to the location. Discuss every possible contingency that could occur during the production so there will be no unresolved differences cropping up during actual production.

Put into writing all agreements, have the site authority sign it, keep a copy, give them a copy, and send a copy to the ultimate authority of the location. Perform this act well before the shoot is scheduled so that any problems can be resolved before the cast and crew arrive for the shoot.

MOUNTAIN PRODUCTIONS
LOCATION RELEASE

I hereby irrevocably grant to __Mountain Productions__ the right to use the property described below which is owned and/or controlled by me at _____
(full legal description of property)
in connection with the production, duplication, and/or distribution of the video, film, or sound recording program, segment, or shots recorded on:

_____ , by <u>Mountain Productions</u>.
(Date)

I hereby assign to <u>Mountain Productions</u> all rights, title, and interest in the materials as they are integrated into the final master film, videotape, or audio recording, granting full and unrestricted permission and authority to <u>Mountain Productions</u> to record, reproduce, and use in any manner, media, or form whatsoever including securing copyrights for the final master and subsequent copies of all media materials produced which includes the image of my property, warranting that I have unrestricted right to make this grant and assignment and hereby release and agree to indemnify and save harmless <u>Mountain Productions</u> , its staff and agents for any and all liability, claims, actions, and damages arising in an manner from the material which contains the image of my property.

For the use of the above described property and the right described in this clearance, <u>Mountain Productions</u> agrees to compensate me as follows: _____ .

I express my intention to be firmly and legally bound this

_____ day of _____ , 19___ .

_____   _____
(Signature)   (Witness)

_____   _____
(Print Name)   (Print Name)

_____   _____
(Street Address)   (Street Address)

_____   _____
(City-State-Zip)   (City-State-Zip)

Site Survey and Location Planning

Be sure to visit the location at the time of day, day of the week, and, if possible, day of the month that the production will be shot. This precautionary act may avoid unplanned traffic, noise, lighting, and ambient-sound problems. Each room or space to be used should be measured accurately, and a scale drawing should be plotted indicating the location and sizes of windows and doors, the furniture placement, and placement of walls and power sources. In addition to the location of power outlets, the location of the fuse or circuit-breaker box should be determined. Discuss with the site authority whether you may tap into the fuse box or if it can be left open in case a fuse or breaker blows so that the crew can correct the problems without waiting for the box to be unlocked or handled by an assigned person. While checking the location of the breaker box, check the power rating of each circuit and try to determine which circuits control specific outlets that you may use.

Once all of the measurements have been taken and the plot is drawn, then possible locations for performers and cameras should be determined. The movements of the performers should be noted as well as camera movements. If furniture needs to be moved or extra furniture or set pieces are required, this should be indicated on the plot. The plot is a scale diagram drawn as if you are looking straight down on the location. It is not drawn in perspective and is useless if not drawn to an accurate scale.

Before leaving the site meeting, determine from the site authority where production vehicles may be safely and legally parked and the location of a loading area. When possible, choose a loading/parking location that is well lit and under some security. If the location does not provide security for vehicles, it may be necessary to hire or provide your own security personnel. If permits for parking and/or loading are required, determine the process and authority for getting such permits. Keep in mind that not even public property can be used for any production purpose without permission, a permit, and often a fee.

Before leaving the site during the survey, recheck all of the information gathered and make certain you have all the facts, permits, measurements, and telephone numbers and that there are no conflicts or contradictions in your lists.

With the completed shooting script and plot in hand, the director can sit down at the site later and determine which shots are to be made from each camera location. The director should indicate on a shooting list (shot sheet) which shots are to be shot at each camera location and the order in which they are to be shot. The most efficient use of cast, crew, and equipment should be the key in this determination. Make certain all possible shots are planned from each location before the camera and lights are moved to the next location.

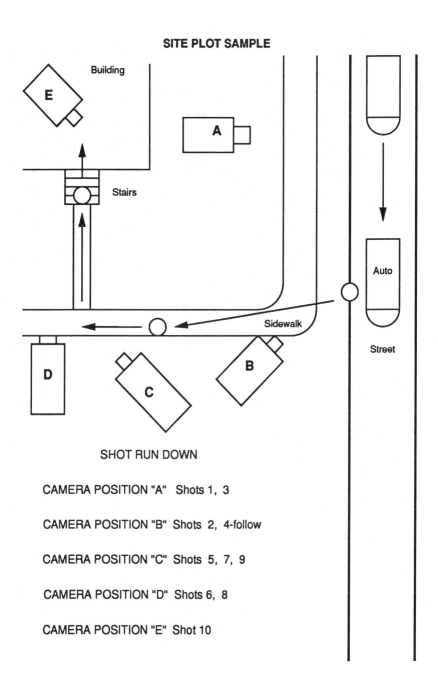

SITE PLOT SAMPLE

Building

E

A

Stairs

Auto

Sidewalk

Street

D

C

B

SHOT RUN DOWN

CAMERA POSITION "A" Shots 1, 3

CAMERA POSITION "B" Shots 2, 4-follow

CAMERA POSITION "C" Shots 5, 7, 9

CAMERA POSITION "D" Shots 6, 8

CAMERA POSITION "E" Shot 10

97

Organizing Equipment

Once the site survey has been completed, the director, camera operator, gaffer, and audio operator meet to list the equipment required for the shoot. These three key crew members should accompany the director on the site survey if at all possible. Each crew chief is responsible for the equipment needed to fulfill his or her responsibilities, but a production meeting should be held to double-check all aspects of the production and for an exchange of ideas, solutions to problems, and resolution of unanswered concerns.

Making a list of equipment will help make certain that everything has been thought of that will be needed. It also may be used as a checklist when packing up the equipment to make certain that nothing has been left behind at the end of the shoot. The director confers with the crew chiefs on the number and skills of crew members required. Most EFP shoots are organized to use a minimum number of people, but the complexity of the production will determine the size of the crew.

Once all the lists are completed, the director and producer work out a detailed schedule that starts with that day and ends with the delivery of the finished product. Each stage of the production needs to be organized on a time line so each stage can proceed unaffected by delays in other stages, if at all possible. But the interdependency of media production makes a time-line schedule critical in the efficient completion of any project.

TIME LINE PLOT

DATE	RESEARCH WRITING	PRE-PROD. SURVEYS	PRODUCTION	POST -PROD.
Jan. 1	Begin research			
Jan. 15	Develop concept			
Feb. 1	Deliver proposal			
Feb. 15	Deliver treatment			
March 1	Compete research			
March 15	Treatment approved			
April 1		Location scouting		
April 15	Scene script approved	Sign location contracts		
May 1	Shooting script approved	Cast-crew equipment contracts		
May 15		Begin rehearsals	Set up for shooting	
June 1				Begin editing
June 15			Complete major videography	
July 30			Pick-up shots	Review rough cut
Aug. 1				
Aug. 15				Deliver answer print
Aug. 30				Deliver completed master

99

Production Stages and Setup

As in each level of the production process, there are four standard stages in the actual shooting of an EFP production: setting up, rehearsing, shooting, and striking.

Setting Up
Assuming all of the preproduction steps were followed, the first step of the production stage is unloading the equipment and moving it to the first shooting location. A word about security: professional video equipment is expensive and looks attractive to thieves. Never leave equipment unguarded, and never leave the production vehicle unlocked.

Move the equipment from the vehicle (unless it is being used as a field control room) efficiently to the first camera setup.

Field Equipment Considerations
Field equipment is much more suceptible to damage and technical problems from the environment than studio equipment. Since the majority of the operating parts are electronic, at a certain level of humidity the equipment becomes inoperative. This is particularly true of tape decks. In addition, keep all liquids away from all electronic equipment. Severely cold weather will slow mechanical works, such as the motors that drive tape decks and zoom lenses. Extreme heat will affect circuits inside the camera and decks and may damage tape stock. In most cases these factors can be compensated for, but they must be taken into consideration when planning a field production.

Camera
Once the camera's position is set, the tripod is set up. Its legs need to be set in a wide enough stance to provide a stable base, but not spread so far apart that they are in the way of traffic or the operator. The height of the tripod is adjusted to be at the eye level of the subject, unless the director requires a special angle.

The head of the tripod should be leveled with the bubble level, and then the camera may be mounted on the head. Make certain the pan and tilt locks are tight, or if the tripod head does not have locks, tighten the drag controls so the camera will not tilt out of control. Set the drag controls tight enough so that there is enough back-pressure to allow for a smooth, even pan or tilt, not so tight as to cause a jerk when you try to pan or tilt. The legs of the tripod should be set so the operator can stand between two legs, not straddling a leg.

100

SETTING UP EQUIPMENT

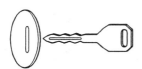

ALWAYS lock the vehicle when leaving expensive equipment unattended.

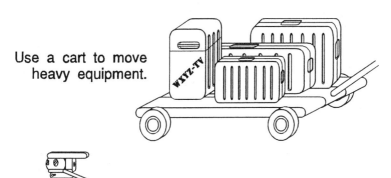

Use a cart to move heavy equipment.

After determining the camera position, set up the tripod.

The tripod head should be "bubble-leveled," and the pan and tilt locks should be tightened.

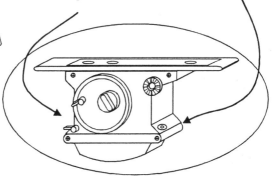

Lighting Preparation

As soon as the crew arrives at the location, the lighting director or gaffer should run the power cable to the camcorder or recorder and then string power cables to the lighting instrument locations. Once the camera is in position, the gaffer can start placing the instruments. Power cables should be run where there is the least amount of foot traffic, out of sight of the camera, yet with as short a run as possible. As mentioned earlier, close consideration must be given to the amount of amperage drawn by the lighting instruments to avoid blowing breakers or fuses.

Proper lighting is an artistic endeavor. While there is much science and practicality to lighting design, lighting is probably the most artistic portion of video production. There are no hard and fast rules, only guidelines. There are typical and traditional setups, but every lighting situation is unique and must be approached from an individualistic direction, depending partially on the director's and writer's concept of the production and partially on the requirements set by the location, budget, and availability of equipment and time to create the lighting ambience desired.

Three types of lighting are basic for EFP productions: realistic, abstract, and neutral. Dramatic productions and some types of commercials require as realistic a lighting setting as possible. Music videos, some commercials, and science fiction dramas may require abstract lighting that goes beyond realism. Neutral lighting is often used for game shows, some newscasts, situation comedies, and some commercials. Hard and fast rules defining each of these types of lighting do not exist, but the end result must match the director's requirements.

In addition to the director's requirements for the lighting—that it set the mood, time, and type of production—the second requirement is that the lighting provide enough base illumination for the camera to create a usable image. As mentioned early in this text, the camera tubes or chips reproduce what is presented to them. The light must be of the correct color and intensity and be within the contrast range of the particular type of camera in use. These three factors control the basic lighting setup. Once these have been satisfied, then creative and innovative lighting techniques may be used.

Types of Lighting

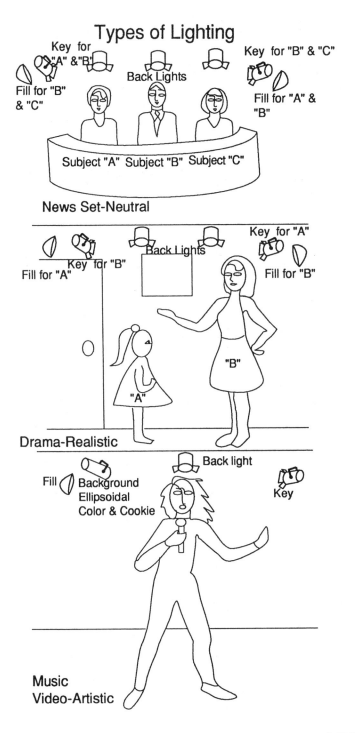

Key for "A" & "B"

Fill for "B" & "C"

Back Lights

Key for "B" & "C"

Fill for "A" & "B"

Subject "A" Subject "B" Subject "C"

News Set-Neutral

Fill for "A"

Key for "B"

Back Lights

Key for "A"

Fill for "B"

"B"

"A"

Drama-Realistic

Fill

Background Ellipsoidal Color & Cookie

Back light

Key

Music Video-Artistic

Controlling Color Temperature

Studio productions control color temperature by installing lamps with the same color temperature output in all lighting fixtures. In the field, controlling color temperature is not as simple or easy. Even though all of the instruments may be lamped with the same Kelvin temperature bulbs, windows, fluorescent lighting fixtures, and even standard incandescent fixtures create a variation in color temperature. If possible, light a set only with lighting instruments lamped with the proper bulbs. Windows should be covered with drapes, blinds, or a large sheet of Wratten 85 (yellow-orange) filter material. This accomplishes two tasks: first, it changes the daylight entering the window to a close equivalent to the 3,200° K lamps, and second, it cuts the intensity of the bright daylight by one or two stops. A second method of lighting with daylight entering a room is to convert the field lighting fixtures to approximate daylight by covering them with Wratten 82 (blue) filter material or a dichroic filter. This will help match the mixed lighting, but will not help balance the difference in light intensity between the daylight and the lighting instruments. This is because the blue filter will reduce the lighting instrument output by about half, requiring more powerful or a greater number of lamps.

If many incandescent fixtures are present and they cannot be covered or turned off, most video cameras' white balance circuits will reach white balance without a filter in place. A very pale blue filter may be necessary to reach true white.

When shooting in a location lit by fluorescent lamps, there are several possible solutions. First, it is sometimes possible to white balance with only the fluorescent lamps by using the daylight (85) filter in the camera. This does reduce the light input, but not radically. If white balance cannot be reached, then the tubes may be covered with a light magenta filter or especially manufactured filters that slip over the fluorescent tubes. Because fluorescents give off a nearly shadowless fill light, it is also possible to light a scene with fairly bright professional tungsten lamps as key lights and over-power the fluorescent fixtures. This is another example of mixed lighting.

COMPENSATING LENS FILTERS

Neutral Density

Light loss	Filter
1/3 stop	.10
2/3 stop	.20
1 stop	.30
1-1/3 stops	.40
1-2/3 stops	.50
2 stops	.60
3 stops	.90

Color Correction

Conversion in degrees Kelvin	Light loss	Filter
3200 to 5400	2 stops	80A
5400 to 3200	2/3 stops	85B
3000 to 3200	1/3 stops	82A

Fluorescent Correction

Light loss	Filter
1/3 stop	CC-05M
2/3 stop	CC-30M

The total light loss with a combination of filters is the sum of the individual losses.

Controlling Light Intensity

In a studio setting the intensity of light is controlled in a variety of ways: by varying the voltage to each instrument through a dimmer board, by adding filters or scrims to the instruments, or by mounting or moving instruments closer or further away from the subject.

In the field, light intensity controls are limited by the types of portable equipment available. These limitations are set by the size and budget of the production. For the average EFP production, simpler means of light control than those used in the studio are necessary

Generally the lighting instruments used in the field are of the open-faced type, which means that the light is harsher and more difficult to control. Using scrims and filters and bouncing the light will soften, diffuse, and lower the light level to that required for fill lights. Key and back-light levels also may be controlled by using scrims and filters.

Small portable dimmers are available for field use, but lowering the voltage of a tungsten lamp changes the color temperature approximately 100° for each 10 V variation. Portable dimmers also tend to be heavy, bulky, and often require an electrician to hook them up to a breaker box for the power required.

The most practical method of controlling light intensity in the field is the placement of the lighting instruments. Since light levels follow the inverse square law, a relatively small movement of a lamp will make a major difference in the light level falling on the subject. If a lamp provides 100 foot candles of light at a distance of 10 feet from the subject, moving the lamp to 5 feet will boost the light level to 400 foot candles, (the inverse square of 1/2 equals 4 times the original light level; therefore, 100 equals 400). If the lamp is moved back to 20 feet, the light level would fall to 25 foot candles (the inverse square of 2 is 1/4 times the original light level of 100, which gives 25 foot candles).

Most EFP lighting directors find they can achieve the light levels and effects the director requires with a combination of lighting instrument placement and the judicious use of scrims, filters, barndoors, and flags.

Lamp Accessories

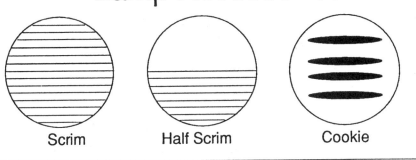

Scrim   Half Scrim   Cookie

Inverse Square Law

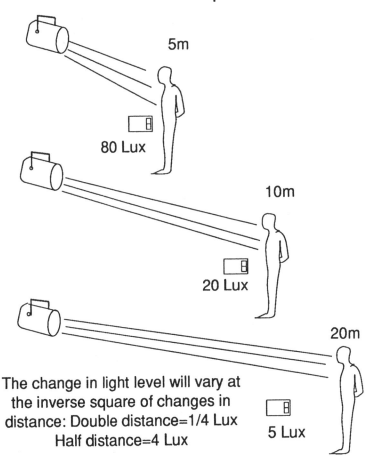

5m

80 Lux

10m

20 Lux

20m

The change in light level will vary at
the inverse square of changes in
distance: Double distance=1/4 Lux
Half distance=4 Lux

5 Lux

107

Contrast Range

The control for contrast is a little more complex. A reflected spot light meter is needed to measure the amount of light reflected from the brightest and darkest objects in the picture. These light measurements are called the reflectance values. The tricky part is that if there are either highly reflective or very dark objects in the frame, these should be excluded from the reading. A judgment must be made as to whether or not it is necessary to reproduce detail in either of those areas. If the amount of light reflected from the brightest portion of the frame in which detail is required reflects more than 30 times the light in the darkest area needed for detail, then additional full light will be needed on the dark areas or some light will have to be taken off the lighter areas. By carefully lighting for the contrast range of the video camera, you can avoid having important areas "bloom" or "flare" into a white mass or having large areas appear so dark and black that they look "muddy."

The most difficult situations for maintaining proper contrast range are those shot in the bright sunlight or at night with available light. During a cloudless bright day, it is nearly impossible to balance the bright sun with any other light source to maintain contrast range. The best method for balancing the lighting is to use the sun as the backlight and reflect the sunlight back toward the subject.

Night lighting is more difficult. Some source of fill is needed to overcome the bright harsh light from street lights, automobile headlights, advertising signs, and other lights. The easiest method is to shoot at dawn or dusk, except that the time period when there is enough light to shoot and still have it look like night is very short. The other method is to shoot day-for-night. This involves white balancing with a yellow instead of a white board and underexposing by two stops or using an 82 (dark blue) filter and underexposing by two stops. In day-for-night shots street lights, auto lights, and other light sources normally on at night must be turned on, even though the scene is actually being shot during the day.

CONTRAST RANGE

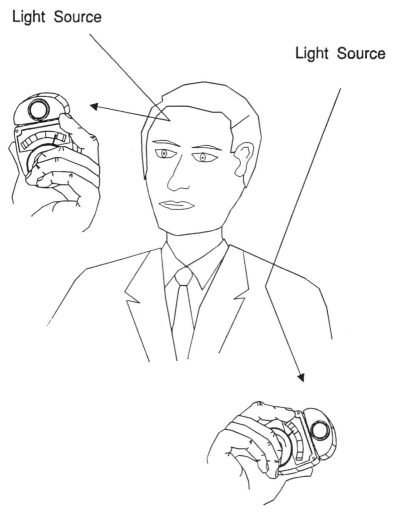

Light Source

Light Source

Establish contrast range by
measuring the amount of
reflected light in the brightest
area versus the amount of
reflected light in the darkest area.

Basic Three-Point Lighting

Lighting practice is based on two suppositions: that there will be enough light for the camera to create a reasonably useful picture and that the appearance will fulfill the "look" that the director desires. *Basic three-point lighting* is designed to satisfy both of these requirements. Three-point lighting derives its name from the three lighting instruments used to achieve satisfactory levels and appearance: key, fill, and back lights. The key light duplicates the major light source in our lives, the sun, and secondarily, the overhead lighting present in most homes and work spaces. The fill light balances the key light, reducing the contrast ratio and softening the harsh look of a one-light source. The back light adds a rim of light around the subject to separate it from the background and add a third dimension to the two-dimensional video field.

Back Light

The *back light* is usually the first instrument set in place since once performers, set pieces, and props are in place it is difficult to reach the proper position for a back light. The next light is the key light; then the fill, kickers, set, and extra lights are set. The back light instrument is mounted above and slightly behind the major subject and directly opposite the camera position. Since this lamp is focused toward the camera, it is necessary to use barndoors or a flag to avoid having the back light shine directly into the lens of the camera.

Key Light

The *key light* is the main source of light. It always should be motivated; that is, there should be a reason for its angle and position. If there is no apparent motivation, then the key should be set about 45 degrees above the camera and from 60 to 40 degrees to one side of the camera. The key should be the brightest light under normal circumstances. It can create shadows, adding depth to the picture, and should set the major color temperature for that shot or scene.

Fill Light

The *fill light* represents the reflected light from clouds, the sky, buildings, and multiple light sources found in buildings. In some ways, it is, like the back light, an artificial light, but it is very important in video production. The fill light should be mounted on the opposite side of the camera from the key, should be of a lower intensity, and should be softer and more diffused and not create any visible shadows.

Basic Lighting Plot
Fixed Single Subject

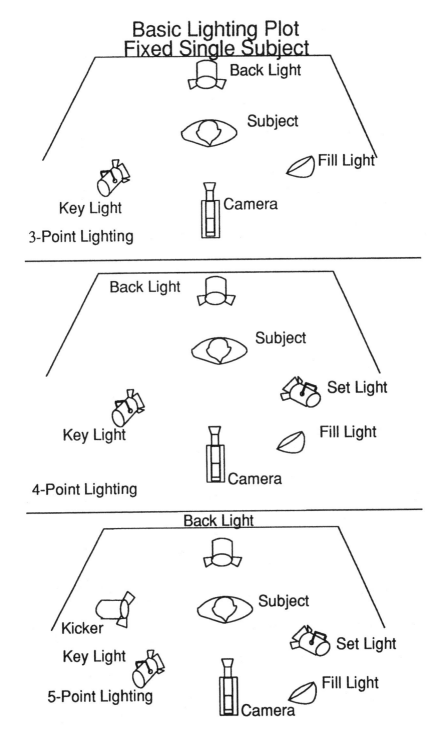

Back Light

Subject

Fill Light

Key Light

Camera

3-Point Lighting

Back Light

Subject

Set Light

Key Light

Fill Light

Camera

4-Point Lighting

Back Light

Subject

Kicker

Set Light

Key Light

5-Point Lighting

Fill Light

Camera

More Complex Lighting

Kicker and Set Lights

A variety of other lighting instruments may be needed to create either realistic light or the effect desired in the scene. The two most common are the kicker and the set light.

The *kicker* is a light mounted to one side of the subject so that it throws its light along the side of the subject. This light acts much like the back light, helping to separate the subject from the background, thus adding depth to the frame.

The *set light* is designed to highlight specific areas of the set. Sometimes it also separates the subject from the set, but more often it is designed to draw attention to particular areas of the set, such as a logo, important set piece, or a lit area of an otherwise dark background.

Multiple and/or Moving Subjects

Lighting a single subject that does not move during the taping is relatively simple. The lighting process becomes complicated when there is more than one subject in the frame and those subjects begin to move about on camera.

Multiple subjects may be lit by spreading the light source wider to take in more than one subject, but this method seldom is satisfactory. Unless both subjects are facing the same direction and are an equal distance from the light source, they will be lit unevenly.

One solution is to *cross-key light;* that is, use the key light for the subject on one side as the fill for the subject on the other side, and vice versa. More than two subjects may require key lights for each subject and a wide-spread series of fill lights covering the entire area. The major problem with multiple key lights is the possibility that the lights will create multiple shadows. The multiple shadows may be avoided by washing out some of the shadows with fill and set lights or by focusing the keys so the shadows fall outside of the area covered by the camera frame.

If subjects move, lighting becomes even more complex. One solution is to arrange key and back lights so that they throw a relatively even pattern of light over the area of movement at an equal distance from the light source. Fill usually is easily flooded out to cover the entire area. Another solution is to break the movement down into several shots. Each shot will cover only a small portion of the movement area and can be more easily lit because the subject can be lit in roughly the same intensity for each shot.

Complex Lighting Plots

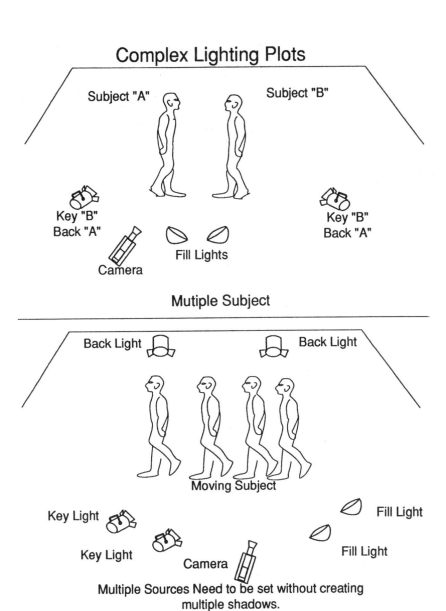

Subject "A"

Subject "B"

Key "B"
Back "A"

Key "B"
Back "A"

Camera

Fill Lights

Mutiple Subject

Back Light

Back Light

Moving Subject

Key Light

Fill Light

Key Light

Fill Light

Camera

Multiple Sources Need to be set without creating multiple shadows.

Creative Lighting

Beyond providing enough light for the camera to produce a usable picture, lighting is also a key creative visual element. Light sets the mood, may be used to indicate the time, the date, and the location of a production.

Mood Lighting
From the first moment an audience sees the opening shots of a situation comedy, they are made aware that they are in for some light-hearted entertainment. Much of that realization comes from the high-key, low-contrast, nearly shadowless lighting used, known as *Notan lighting*. This term came from Japanese artists who painted brightly lit scenes without any shadows. The brightly lit set without any dark areas lets the audience know what mood the director wishes them to feel.

On the other hand, should the first shot of a scene be lit with low-key, high-contrast, heavy, dark shadows, the audience is made aware that this is a heavy drama. This type of lighting is called *Chiaroscuro*, borrowed from the Italian painters who used the same high contrast to set the mood of their paintings. The lighting (and probably the set, costumes, coloring, and mannerism of the actors) gives the audience the advance information that they probably will not spend much time laughing during this scene. Of course, all creative techniques may be used in contrast; that is, a comedy scene may be lit in low key to make it funnier because it is unexpected.

Lighting for time, date, location
Using lighting to indicate time, date, and location is a little more subtle but should always be taken into consideration when designing a scene. Early morning and late afternoon light is different from that at high noon. The colors are different (early and late in the day the light is warmer, redder), and the angle of the light is lower. Winter sun is bluer and colder, and that of the summer, fall, and spring each has its own colors and contrast levels. A setting in the tropics will have a higher key light than that of a northern European city or a slum setting.

Light may also be used simply as an abstract creative object in and of itself. Light slashes across the background will provide a feeling of prison bars, window slats, venetian blinds, or other settings not actually present. *Cukaloris patterns* on a plain background will tell the audience an infinite number of characteristics about a scene. A cukaloris is a metal disk inserted into an ellipsoidal spotlight that creates a light pattern or mottled design on the background.

Each location should be carefully analyzed for the proper light level, angle, color, and contrast settings to fit with the intended feeling desired by the director.

Ellipsoidal Spot and Cukaloris (cookie) Patterns

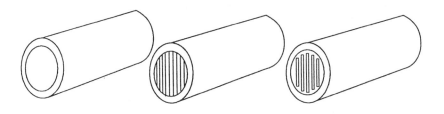

Lamp Position

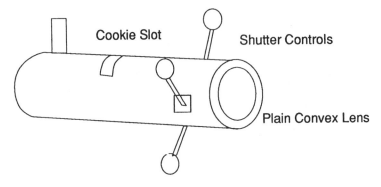

Cookie Slot

Shutter Controls

Plain Convex Lens

Sets and Properties

For most field productions, sets and properties (props) exist at the location chosen. The convenience of using already existing rooms, furniture, and other props may be one of the main reasons for shooting a production in the field. At the same time, a careful and well-thought-out choice of a location is critical in the field production process.

There are three levels of items in this category: sets, set pieces, and hand props. *Sets* are backgrounds. They may be actual walls, trees, constructions made of cloth or wood, or simply the actual location suitable for the particular production. *Set pieces* are items attached to or placed within a set. Generally, set pieces include paintings on walls, furniture, automobiles, or bookcases. *Hand props* are items small enough to be picked up and handled, but for the most part, they are items that need to be handled by the talent during the production.

Choices in each of the categories are made by the director and art director. They should match the tone, time period, quality, and attitude of the production. A beautiful painting should not hang in a set that is supposed to be a dingy office. At the same time, a cheap, poorly done painting should not be seen hanging in a room that is supposed to be the office of a Fortune 500 CEO. These choices must be made on the basis of knowledge of art, architecture, and interior design.

As in lighting design, *set design* sends a clearly defined message to the audience and must match the rest of the production to avoid confusing and misleading the audience. The set design decision should be made during preproduction planning, but often cannot be made until the setup period with the crew on location. Rearranging furniture, rehanging paintings, and removing unnecessary or conflicting items from a room being used as a location site should be accomplished during the setup period.

SET DRESSINGS

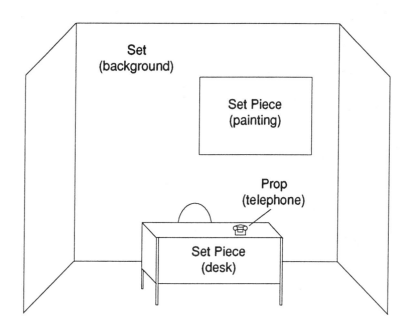

Set
(background)

Set Piece
(painting)

Prop
(telephone)

Set Piece
(desk)

Sets are backgrounds & walls

Set Pieces are furniture & decorative items

Props are items handled by performers

Setting Up the Audio

While the camera operator and gaffer are setting up their equipment, the audio operator is stringing mike cables or setting up the receivers for wireless mikes. If a mixer is used, then the cables need to be strung to the mixer and the output of the mixer to the recorder or camcorder. Levels are checked to make certain the entire audio system is operating and is balanced.

If a boom mike is used, then its position needs to be checked with the camera operator, lighting director, and director. If body mikes are used, the operator needs to place them on the performers, show them how to turn them on, and check to be sure a signal at the proper level is being received at the mixer or recorder.

The audio operator is responsible for all sound. If playback audio is required, then the audio operator must set up the speakers, cables, and audio source, such as a tape deck, CD player, or turntable. If the production involves live music, then the audio operator has the much greater responsibility of miking the band, soloists, or other music sources.

Prompting

Often some type of *prompting* device is needed, especially for commercial shoots. There are three basic types of prompters: hand-held, camera-mounted, and in-ear devices.

Hand-held prompters are pieces of poster board bearing either the entire copy lettered in large bold type or an outline of key words that the performer ad-libs around. These cards have been called *idiot cards* in deference to the talent.

The most common prompting device today consists of monitors mounted above or below the camera lens with two angled mirrors reflecting the monitor image directly in front of the camera lens. This gives the audience the impression that the talent is looking directly at them, but in reality the performer is looking at the image of the copy reflected from a mirror mounted in front of the camera lens. The source of the copy can be scripts that are taped together in a continuous sheet and passed under a black and white camera, or from a dedicated prompter computer or character generator.

The third method requires a special skill on the part of the performer. A small headset is placed in the ear of the performer and a recording of the copy, previously made by the talent, is played back in the ear of the performer. Skilled announcers can repeat vast amounts of their own words slightly delayed from the original as if they were speaking from memory.

Of course, the best option is having a performer who has taken the time and trouble to memorize all of his or her lines.

118

Prompting Devices

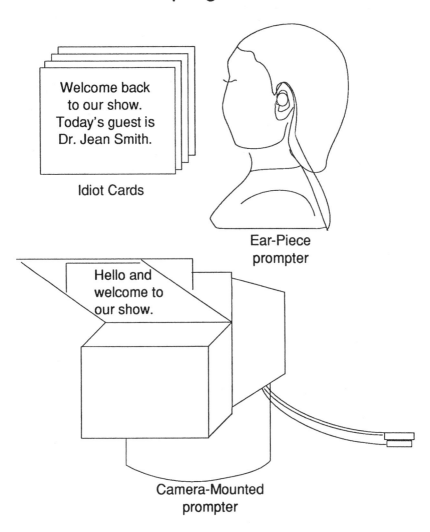

Welcome back
to our show.
Today's guest is
Dr. Jean Smith.

Idiot Cards

Ear-Piece
prompter

Hello and
welcome to
our show.

Camera-Mounted
prompter

Rehearsing and Preparing Talent

While the crew is setting up equipment, the director works with the talent and supervises all of the other operations. The director also checks on all sets, props, prompting devices, and other materials to be used in the first sequence. The setup period blends into the rehearsal period, but actual rehearsal cannot take place until cameras, lights, and microphones are in place and the crew has received preliminary production instructions. Those instructions should include a written sheet for each crew member or crew section. The lighting director and key grip receive the instructions if a full crew is used, the gaffer and grip if there is one crew member for each position.

For the lighting and stage crew, a plot shows the position of the camera for each setup, talent positions and movements, key furniture, and backgrounds or other set pieces. The camera operator receives a shot sheet listing the camera positions in the order of setup and shots to be completed at each camera position in the order they will be shot. A plot also is helpful for the camera operator.

During setup, the director should make certain that all performers are present, in make-up and costume, and prepared to shoot their scenes. General discussions may be carried on about movements, line delivery, motivation, and relationships between actors and other objects while the crew is completing the setup process.

Once the location is ready, the director walks the actors through their starting locations, blocking, and movements, if there are any. The director has the camera operator watch the blocking rehearsal so that he or she can visualize the camera movements needed for each shot. At this time the actors also should deliver their lines with mikes properly placed so the audio operator can set levels and determine if any audio problems exist.

The director plays the role of benevolent dictator to the cast and crew. He or she must have absolute control, but at the same time must respect and listen to the members of the crew for the benefit of their knowledge and expertise. No crew or cast member should argue with the director, but a professional difference of opinion leading to a discussion is permissible if there is time for one. At the end of the discussion, the director's decision is final and must be accepted by all of the cast and crew as such without rancor or spite. The director's decision should be based on his or her knowledge of the entire production, not on the relatively narrow view each cast and crew member might hold.

Once a walk-through rehearsal has been successfully held, several camera rehearsals should be run. This involves everyone on the cast and crew completing their roles as if the shot were being taped. Once the director is satisfied with the performance of both cast and crew, then a take is ordered by the director.

120

LIGHTING PLOT AND SHOT RUNDOWN

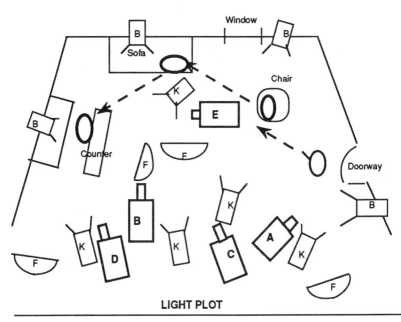

LIGHT PLOT

Shot Rundown

Camera "A" Shots 1, 12

Camera "B" Shots 3, 5, 7, 9

Camera "C" Shots 4, 6, 8

Camera "D" Shots 10, 14

Camera "E" Shot   11

Plot Key

Camera

Key light

Fill Light

Back Light

Talent

Shooting a Scene

The actual process for shooting a take is as follows: the director calls for quiet on the set by calling out "Quiet" or "Stand-by." At that command, complete silence is expected from all cast and crew persons. If the shoot is at a public location, a crew person may have to circulate through the adjacent crowd and quiet them unless the crowd noise is part of the audio ambience. At the "Stand-by" cue, all cast and crew assume their starting positions and prepare physically and mentally for the beginning of the shot.

When the director feels everyone is ready he or she calls, "Roll tape," "Roll it," or maybe even "Roll 'em." As soon as the tape deck is up to speed, either the camera operator, if a camcorder is being used, or the tape operator, if a separate recorder is being used, calls out "Speed" or "Locked in." The director performs a 5-second count, either silently or out loud, and then calls "Action." This 5-second delay is necessary to make certain the tape deck has recorded at least five seconds of clean sync and control track or time code, which is needed for editing purposes. Professional actors will pause a beat and then start their movement or lines. The crew will follow the action as directed during rehearsals.

During a take, there are three people who may shout "Cut." The major responsibility lies with the director, but either the camera operator or the audio operator also may cut a shot. If the camera operator sees in the viewfinder a visual error bad enough to make the take unusable, he or she may yell "Cut." It is best to quickly consult with the director before doing so in case the audio portion of that take is usable even though the video is not. The audio operator has the same responsibility in monitoring the recorded audio. If a noise is present that makes the take unusable, the audio operator also may call "Cut," but once again, because there is always a chance the video is usable, the audio operator should not cut the take without a quick conference with the director. An audio operator seldom will cut a take since most audio can be looped or rerecorded in a Foley session during postproduction if necessary. A Foley session is a special postproduction sound effects session during which all of the various ambiant and replacement sounds are created to match the action of the production.

During both rehearsals and actual recording, standardized electronic media communication hand cues and signals should be used.

HAND CUES

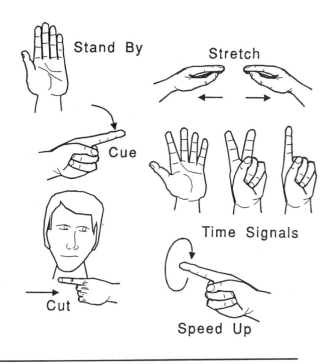

Stand By

Stretch

Cue

Time Signals

Cut

Speed Up

DIRECTOR'S VERBAL CUES

STAND BY   This is a call for quiet on the set or location, especially from the cast and crew. It means they must give the director their undivided attention and wait for the next cue.

ROLL TAPE   This is the cue to the tape or camera operator to start tape rolling and recording, and must be followed by --

SPEED (By the tape or camera operator)
This cue indicates to the director that the tape is rolling and recording, up to speed and locked in, ready for the call for action.

ACTION   This indicates to both the cast and crew to start their rehearsed action, speech, movement, etc.

CUT   This cue means to stop recording, acting, or any other action. It is an indication from the director that either the required material has been recorded or that something has gone wrong and to continue would be a waste of time.

123

Directing Talent

Once all of the physical setup procedures have begun, the director then concentrates on the human values that make up a production. Actual direction of actors is the most complex part of a director's job. The performance of an actor depends on many variables beyond the director's control. An actor's training, background, experience, (both in acting and in life), and mental state during the shoot all affect a performance. First of all, the director must get to know as many of the above factors as is possible in the short time usually available on an EFP shoot. The director must then blend this knowledge with the results of an in-depth study of the script and the plan the director has for how to accomplish his or her interpretation of that script.

Interpersonal communication is the key to working with actors, who are in a very vulnerable position. It is their faces and voices that will be viewed by the audience. If the production comes off poorly, it is actors that the audience will remember. A director must clearly communicate to the actor exactly what is needed, how it fits into the overall production, and how the actor will look and sound. The more precise the direction, for most actors, the better the performance. Without being condescending, a parent–child relationship is often most workable between a director and an actor.

Getting an emotional performance is the most difficult for both the director and the actor. Once again, the actor must trust the director's judgment on how far to go in showing the type of emotion needed for a particular shot or scene. Often actors are not aware that their reaction to other performers is as important as their own actions. This is the type of information a good director will impart to an actor as needed. Without delving into various acting schools and methods, actors perform better if they are aware of why they are doing what they have been asked to do. Supplying this motivation makes their job much easier and their acting generally much more realistic.

ACTOR - DIRECTOR RELATIONSHIP

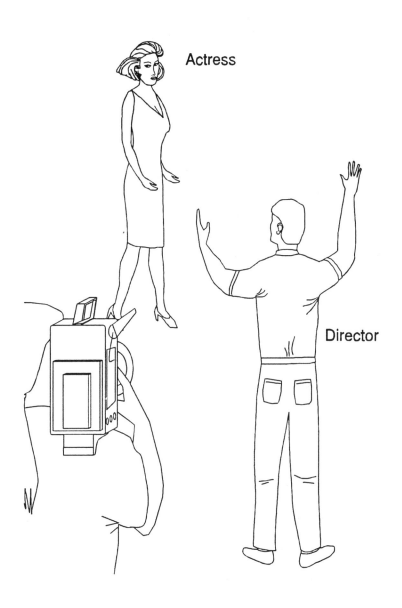

Actress

Director

Shooting and Framing

A relationship of trust and communication must also exist between the director and camera operator, only this time, the trust runs in the opposite direction. The director must trust the camera operator to frame, focus, and expose the shot as the director wanted it shot. Detailed communication from the director to the camera operator provides the best first step toward accomplishing that relationship. If the camera operator understands what the director wants and needs in a shot, sequence, or scene, he or she is better equipped to provide it.

Standard Shot Names

Over the years, starting with motion pictures, the different placements of objects in the field of the camera, called *framing*, have acquired specific names. As in every aspect of media production, there are some variations in these names; nevertheless, the following definitions are accepted and understood by all professionals:

The angle of view varies from the narrowest angle (tightest shot) called an *extreme* or *extra close-up*, abbreviated ECU or XCU. A wider angle is a *close-up* (CU); continuing wider: *medium close-up* (MCU), *medium shot* (MS), *wide shot* (WS), and *extreme* or *extra-wide shot*, (EWS or XWS), the widest shot. Some directors call shots by specific framing: a head-to-toe shot is always an MCU. Others prefer to make their shot variations in reference to the widest and or narrowest shot. For example, in a football game, a shot of the entire field from a blimp obviously would be an XWS, and a shot of the quarterback from the waist up would be an XCU. However, in a television commercial where a football player holds a product in his hand, the XWS would be a head-to-toe shot, and the XCU would be the shot of the label of the product.

Other names of shots are derived from the objects included in the field of view. A *two-shot* contains two objects, usually two people; a *three-shot*, three objects. An *over-the-shoulder* (OS) is a typical news interview shot in which part of the interviewer's shoulder appears in the foreground and the person being interviewed faces the camera. A *point-of-view* (POV) shot appears to be what someone in the scene is actually seeing from their position in the set.

An entire set of shots is called for by their relative framing on the human body: *head shot*, *bust shot*, or *waist shot*. One caution on this type of nomenclature. No shot should cut objects off at logical cut-off points. If a human head is framed so that the bottom of the frame cuts off the head at the neck, it will appear in the shot that the person has been decapitated. It is better to include just a small portion of the shoulders to indicate that the body continues.

126

Shot Framing

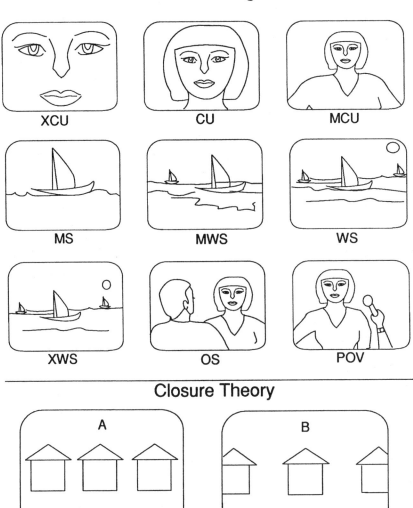

XCU

CU

MCU

MS

MWS

WS

XWS

OS

POV

Closure Theory

A

B

Frame "A" indicates three houses are present.
Frame "B" indicates more than three house.

Framing Principles I

Aspect Ratio

Until a new standard has been agreed upon universally, the standard frame ratio is 3 units high by 4 units wide. This means that to fill the video frame without exceeding its boundaries, the subject must fit into a horizontal rectangle 75 percent wider than it is high. This is an absolute. Turning the camera on its side to frame a predominately tall, slender subject results in an image that is lying on its side.

On the surface this does not seem to offer much of a problem to a director or camera operator, but in reality there are very few objects that fit neatly into 3 x 4 space. Either some of the object must be cut off, or additional items must be added to the picture to create an acceptable composition. The 3 x 4 ratio becomes especially critical when shooting people. Unless it is lying down, the human body does not fit into a 3 x 4 horizontal rectangle; neither does an automobile, most tall buildings, a ship, an airplane, or any number of other everyday objects.

128

Aspect Ratio

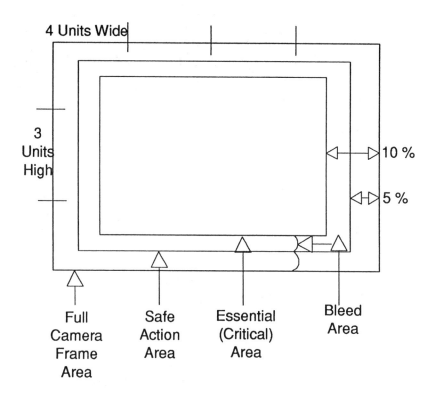

4 Units Wide

3 Units High

10 %

5 %

Full Camera Frame Area

Safe Action Area

Essential (Critical) Area

Bleed Area

Framing Principles II

Critical Area

Besides the 3 x 4 horizontal aspect ratio, an additional framing problem exists in video. All of the video signal created by the camera does not reach the television receiver or monitor, and, in addition, the scanning sweeps of most receivers have increased due to age or misalignment. This means that as much as 10 to 15 percent of the picture cannot be seen by the audience. The 80 percent of the center portion of the frame is considered the critical or essential area. This 80 percent (allowing a 10 percent border on all four sides) is accepted by the industry as the critical area standard. All important information—names, addresses, phone numbers, prices—always should be framed well within the critical area to make certain that all viewers will receive it.

Any objects framed in the 10 percent border may be seen by some viewers, so unwanted objects should not be framed in this area, which is the *edge bleed area*. For sports or other action-oriented coverage, the acceptable framing limitations are a little broader than the critical area, allowing approximately a 5 percent border. The difference in philosophy is that in an action sequence, closure will fill in any portions of objects that momentarily appear beyond the critical area.

"Lead Room" or "Edge Attraction"

Psychological studies indicate that objects in the area near the edge of the frame create a different perception than those in the center of the frame. A major factor is what is called *edge attraction theory*, in which an object appears to move toward the edge even if it remains stationary in the frame. This effect is increased when the object near the edge is a person's face. This lack of "nose" room makes the audience uncomfortable and should be avoided. The attraction of the edge is compounded when the subject is moving toward the edge. That is why moving objects should be given plenty of space ahead of them as the camera follows them on a pan or tilt.

The Rule of Thirds

Related to the edge attraction theory is the artist's *rule of thirds*, which states that the most aesthetic location for a predominately vertical form is one third of the way in from either the left or right side of the frame. Conversely, a predominately horizontal figure's most aesthetic position is either one third of the way up from the bottom or down from the top of the frame. A quick review of the classic art works shows these framing rules are used extensively.

SUBJECT FRAMING RULES

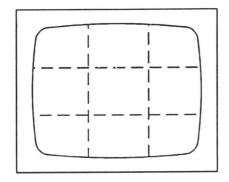

Rule of Thirds

Nose Room

Lead Room

131

Creating Movement I

Even though video is a moving art form, the individual frame is essentially a still photograph. The manner in which each picture is framed can add or subtract to its perceived movement. There are three basic means of creating movement in either video or film: by moving the subject, by moving the camera, and by editing. Within each of these three basic movements are ancillary movements.

Subject movement
Subjects can move in three directions within the frame: on the horizontal (X axis) and vertical (Y axis) planes in front of the camera or moving toward or away (Z axis) from the camera. The Z axis is the most powerful and should be used judiciously. Moving from left to right in our culture suggests moving ahead, and conversely, moving to the left signifies returning or backing up.

The Y axis movements are more complex and less universally accepted, except that movement from the upper left to the lower right implies the most powerful movement forward except for straight toward the camera.

Interestingly, the cultural values attributed to these movements also affect the relative value of positions within the frame. If the frame is divided into nine areas—upper left, upper center, upper right, middle left, center, middle right, lower left, lower center, and lower right—the position considered the most beneficial for passing information to the audience is the lower right. That conclusion is based on the philosophy that in our culture the eye starts at the upper left and proceeds to the lower right and will come to rest there. For that reason ego-centered television program hosts usually insist on being framed on the right, better newscasts place the visuals on the right, and, almost universally, prices, addresses, and other critical commercial information are framed on the right.

Frame Axis

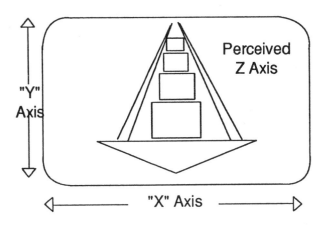

Dominate Movement

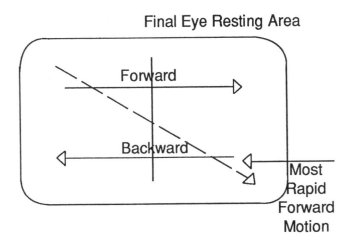

Creating Movement II

Camera Movement

The second means of creating movement is by moving the camera: on its pan head, panning left or right, or tilting up or down. If the camera has a means of raising or lowering on a center shaft, this movement is called *pedestaling up* or *down*. Whether the camera base is a tripod on dolly wheels, a pedestal mount with wheels, a wheeled dolly, crab, or crane mount, the movements may be a dolly in or out, a truck left or right, or a combination of both to move in an arc. The crane mount also permits additional combinations of movement up, down, in, out, left, and right.

Movement Through Zooms

A supplementary movement created within the lens is the zoom. A *zoom movement* is created by varying the focal length of the lens, increasing or decreasing the angle of view. The zoom, especially with a motorized control, is a very easy and flexible movement. But it is an unrealistic movement and should be used with great caution. Amateur videographers use the zoom instead of advance planning and some of the many other aspects of professional video production open to those who have studied and learned to use them.

The zoom does not change the perspective of a shot, so that as the angle narrows and the picture appears to become larger, the camera's angle is not closer. Instead, it is showing a smaller portion of the picture. A dolly would achieve the same movement, but would be more realistic because as the camera moved closer to the subject, the perspective would also change. Although even the most professional film and video camera operators now use zoom lenses, they do not use them during a shot. Instead they will use the zoom lens as it was intended to be used, as a means of varying the focal length of the lens without changing lenses.

Zooms during a shot may be used on a flat, two-dimensional object since there is no perspective involved, or as a special effect. But like all special effects, a zoom should be used sparingly and with specifically planned intent other than just tightening or loosening a shot.

CAMERA MOVEMENTS

 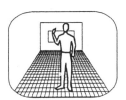 

Panning to the right

Dollying to the right

Tilting up

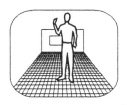  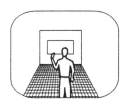

Pedestaling up

135

Creating *Z*-Axis Movement

Video—like painting, photography, and cinematography—is a two-dimensional art form. There exists only a height and width to the picture as received on a receiver/monitor or shown on a screen. The depth, or third dimension, of the picture is perceived; it does not actually exist as a third dimension, but it appears to exist. This 3-D appearance is important to any visual medium. Video particularly depends on the *Z* axis to compensate for its smaller screen and lower resolution as compared to photography or motion picture film.

Therefore, it is imperative that the camera operator and director specifically think about and design the shots so that the *Z* axis is exploited to its maximum. Using all of the creative techniques disclosed in the preceding sections furnishes the means to do so.

Moving subjects in the frame or moving the camera around the subjects, arranging the objects in patterns that appear to be in perspective, using as short a focal length lens as possible, and arranging objects and subjects in the frame to create a background, middle ground, and foreground all help create a usable *Z* axis. Lining up objects in front of the camera in neat rows equal distance from the camera and placing all objects on surfaces of the same height, size, and/or color decrease the appearance of the *Z* axis.

Arranging objects in the frame so that, even at rest, there appears to be movement—by utilizing the object's graphic forces—also improves the third dimension perception. Do not shoot a person or object straight on. This is not only boring, but it adds pounds and width to that person. Instead, rotate the actor so the camera is getting a three-quarter view, but don't turn them so far that both eyes are no longer visible. Avoid having two people stand next to each other talking to the camera or each other; place them so they are facing each other, with the camera shooting past first one and then the other.

136

Z-AXIS DO'S & DON'TS

Graphic Forces

Another aesthetic theory that should be considered when framing a shot is the *graphic weight* of the objects within the frame. Each discernible object has some graphic weight or value. A large, dark object has a greater value than a small, light-colored object. An object with jagged, irregular edges has more weight than an object with smooth, rounded edges. Two small objects may equal the weight of one large one, even though their actual square measurement might be slightly smaller.

In addition to the perceived graphic weight of an object is its *graphic force*. The graphic force is derived partially from its graphic weight, but also from its movement. An object at rest has less graphic force than an object moving across the frame. An object or series of objects that appear to be moving also have increased graphic weight. Objects shaped like an arrow, a row of objects arranged to lead the eye in a specific direction, or a series of shots that show an object in a position of potential movement all carry more graphic force than an object the same size without the same graphic forces present.

In the midst of all these "rules," one cannot forget that there are no absolutes in any aesthetic field. All of the suggestions made in this section are intended to be used only as guidelines. Each individual production situation will determine to what extent these suggestions are followed or ignored. The resulting final production will chronicle whether the best choices were made.

Graphic Forces

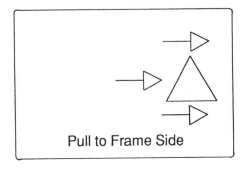

Pull to Frame Side

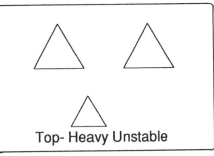

Top- Heavy Unstable

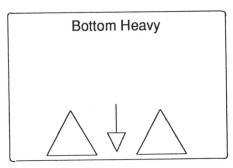

Bottom Heavy

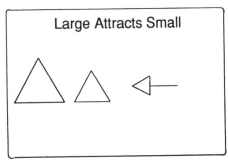

Large Attracts Small

Shooting to Edit: The Third Movement

Regardless of the skill of the camera operator and director in planning and framing shots, unless the shots have been recorded to be edited together, all of the aesthetic values will be lost. In EFP production, each shot is recorded separately, often out of order. To be able to assemble the shots in a meaningful manner close to the original intent of the production, they must be shot with editing in mind.

First, the *electronic aspect* must be considered. Because electronic editors require some preroll space before making an edit, there must be at least 5 seconds of uninterrupted sync pulses and control track pulses (if it is a CT editor) preceding the edit entry point. This means that after the director has called for the tape to roll, a full 5 seconds must elapse before any usable action is recorded. At the end of the take another 5 seconds ought to be recorded as protection after the director has called "Cut."

Second, the *practical aspect*. Each shot should be recorded so that its action overlaps both the preceding and following shot. This allows the editor greater protection in case a shot did not start or end exactly as intended.

Third, the *aesthetic aspect*. In order to edit in a seamless fashion, continuity must be maintained. The action from one shot must flow into the action of the next, unless there is a transition or change of scene. In order to avoid discontinuity problems, shots are recorded overlapping each other to offer the editor a choice in where to make the edit. There are three basic types of continuity that generally must be matched in each edit: action, direction, and location.

EDITING PATTERNS

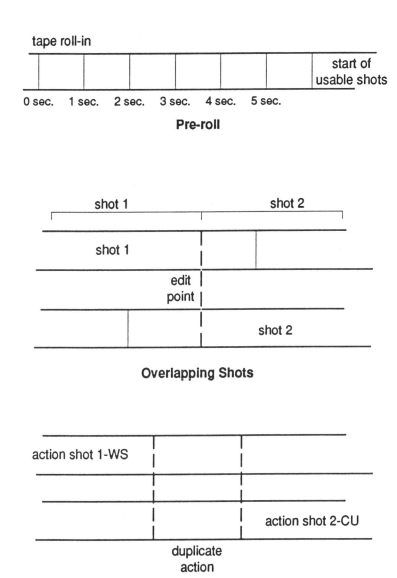

tape roll-in

						start of usable shots

0 sec.　1 sec.　2 sec.　3 sec.　4 sec.　5 sec.

Pre-roll

shot 1　　　　　　shot 2

shot 1

edit
point

shot 2

Overlapping Shots

action shot 1-WS

action shot 2-CU

duplicate
action

Maintaining Continuity

The Three Types of Continuity

Continuity of Action

As the actor picks up the pencil in the WS, the CU must be shot so that the rate of picking up the pencil is the same and the same hand and pencil are used.

Continuity of Direction

If the WS shows the actor facing to the left, and his or her right hand reaches across the frame to the left, then the CU must show the hand moving to the left. If a shot shows an actor moving to the right, then the next shot must show the same actor still moving to the right unless there is a change of direction shown on camera in the shot or a cutaway is inserted between the two shots. This last can even confuse the audience, however, if they remember that the actor was moving in one direction and the next time he or she is seen moving in the opposite direction. A straight-on shot from directly in front or from the rear of the actor also can be used as a transition. This same rule applies to all movement whether it involves automobiles; airplanes; people walking, running, or falling; or objects being thrown, dropped, or moving on their own.

Continuity of Location

Continuity of location includes lighting, background, and audio. If the establishing shot is lit in low key with heavy shadows, then all of the CUs must also be lit the same way. If one shot shows the ocean in the background, then unless there is a change of direction shown on camera, all shots should indicate the ocean is the background. Audio continuity becomes an aesthetic tool as well as a continuity rule. If the scene is in a large empty hall, all of the audio must sound as if it were recorded in the same ambience. However, the ambience of a wide shot in the same location will sound different from that of a tight CU of two people talking and standing close to each other.

SHOOTING FOR EDITING

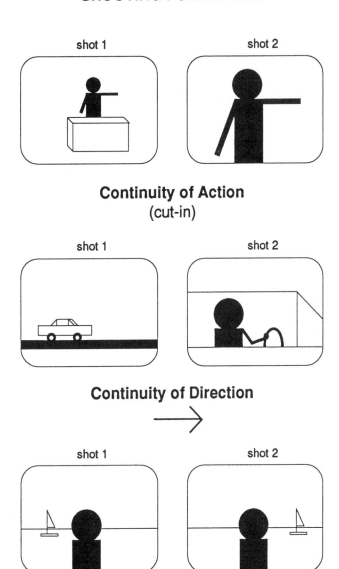

Continuity of Action
(cut-in)

Continuity of Direction

Continuity of Location

143

Cover Shots

There are three types of shots, called *cover shots*, that are the friends and saviors of the editor. Any capable director will call for them to be recorded, and any professional camera operator will shoot them even if the director forgets to do so.

These shots are called *cover, cut-away,* and *cut-in shots.* A cover shot is an illustration of what is being talked about or referred to. If an announcer speaks of the use of a product, then a shot of the product being used in that manner would be a cover shot. The announcer does not need to appear in the shot.

Cut-away and cut-in shots are similar, except that a cut-away is a shot of items that are not included in the previous or following shots: For example, when two people are sitting talking in a railway station and a shot of the train is shown arriving. They do not refer to it (if they did, it would be a cover shot), and most importantly, they must be sitting so they are not included in the shot of the train.

A cut-in is a close-up of some object that is visible in the preceding or following frame. If a CU of the women's purse is used as the two sit in the train station, it is cut-in if the purse is visible in the WS.

These three types of shots afford the editor the chance to correct mistakes made in the shooting continuity or can be used as a means of speeding up or slowing down a sequence or correcting a continuity problem in the production.

COVER SHOTS

Cover

Cut-away

Cut-in

In-Camera Effects I

The technology exists that allows for the production of a series of special effects simply by utilizing the controls necessary for the normal operation of a camera. Depending on the quality and level of the recorder, some effects may be produced by its operation. As technology advances, newer cameras are being produced that have digital special effects capabilities built into them.

Six effects may be produced with almost any professional camera: iris fades, rack focus, swish pans/zooms, reverse polarity, and manipulation of pedestal and gain, including electronic fades.

Iris Fades

An *iris fade-in* or *-out* is created by placing the iris control on manual and setting the iris opening stopped all the way down. With the tape rolling, the iris may be slowly opened up and brought to the proper setting. This creates a fade-in. A fade-out may be created by reversing the procedure: a scene is started with the tape rolling and the iris set properly. At the right moment, the iris is stopped down until the picture fades to black. Neither of these effects works well unless the light level is low enough so that the iris is nearly wide open at the proper setting.

Rack Focus

To *rack focus* simply means to start a scene in focus and rapidly turn the focus control until the picture is totally out of focus. The shot to be edited next should start totally out of focus and, on cue, roll into proper focus. Once again, neither of these effects works well unless the light level is low enough so that the depth of field is quite shallow.

Swish Pans and Zooms

A *swish pan* is accomplished by starting on a scene and at the end of the shot, quickly panning the camera at a high enough rate that the image is blurred. The next shot starts with a fast pan and ends properly framed. The first of these is easy to accomplish, but for the second, it is very difficult to stop at the exact framing without jerking or missing the mark.

A *swish zoom* is a little easier, especially if the zoom is motorized. The process is the same as a swish pan in that the shot starts at a normal focal length and, on cue, the zoom control is operated at its maximum speed, usually zooming in rather than out. The second shot starts with a zoom out and ends properly framed.

146

IN-CAMERA EFFECTS

Swish Pan

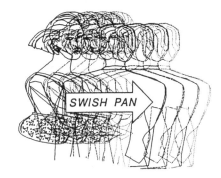

beginning of shot A

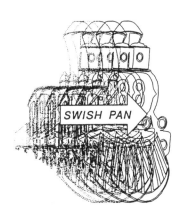

end of shot B

In-Camera Effects II

Pedestal and Variable Gain Manipulation

Two other electronic controls, usually located internally on the camera, are the pedestal and variable gain controls. All cameras have a *gain control* easily located on the outside of the camera, but it is a step switch that gives the operator a choice of setting several different gain levels in the video amplifier. This switch allows the operator to compensate for low light levels by boosting the gain internally. Although the gain boost makes the picture brighter, it also increases the noise level in the picture.

The *internal gain control* is a potentiometer that allows continuous gain settings. If an iris fade is not possible, slowly decreasing the gain can produce a fade-out. Starting with the gain turned down and bringing it up on cue results in a fade-in. The pedestal control changes the black level or contrast of the picture. A caution on the manipulation of either the pedestal or internal gain controls: Once either of these controls has been changed, it probably will require a test signal, oscilloscope, and a technician to return the camera to its normal operating condition; therefore, this should be done only under extreme production needs.

Reversing Polarity

Reversing polarity is achieved by throwing a switch, on some cameras internally and on others externally. This cannot be done while you are recording as there is a momentary loss of sync. The picture areas that were red become cyan, those that were green become magenta, and blue areas become yellow, and vice versa. Light areas become dark; dark areas, light. The effect is the same as looking at a color film negative.

Other In-Camera Effects

If the camera has built-in digital circuits, it may be possible to solarize, freeze, or pixilate the picture. The solarization effect appears as if the picture is melting or reversing in polarity. A freeze effect locks a single frame of the picture as if it were a still photo, and pixilation is the process of removing a certain number of frames of the picture so that objects and subjects appear to move about in an irregular, jerky fashion. Each of these effects requires a separate control on the camera to produce the indicated effect. Pixilation also may be accomplished if the tape deck can record a single frame at a time. A control, usually labeled *intervalometer*, sets the number of frames per second the recorder will operate. This then compresses the action in any time elapsed required for the production.

All of these effects can be accomplished better through a camera unit or in postproduction.

CAMERA CONTROL EFFECTS

Solarization

normal picture

solarized picture

Continuity Records: Logging

A manual operation often overlooked in the concentration on electronic operations in a video production is the continuity record keeping or logging process. A written record of each shot is kept on a log sheet in a form that supplies the director and editor with the information they need to accomplish their tasks. The log registers in the order of shooting the shot and take number, location on the tape (tape counter or SMPTE time code number), comments on whether the take audio and/or video was a good or bad take and usually why, and any other comments the director wanted noted at the time.

The log is invaluable to the editor. If not accurately logged during the shot, the tape reels have to be previewed and logged in the postproduction process, which is a slow and painstaking procedure. The logs should be kept by one person, and that should be his or her main responsibility. The person's title in a large crew is "continuity assistant" or "secretary"; in a smaller crew, the director or an assigned production assistant will be in charge of logging. The importance of this function cannot be ignored. The person keeping the log must be familiar with the critical aspects of continuity and well versed in that particular production.

The continuity assistant (CA) will have a copy of the shot sheet indicating the order in which the shots will be set up and recorded, as well as a copy of the latest revision of the script. It is helpful to the log keeper to have been present at the production meetings held previous to the shoot to become intimately aware of all aspects of the production.

As each shot is set up and rehearsed, the logger notes positions of props, set pieces, lighting, or anything else that may be moved or changed. Since the production will be shot out of sequence, there may be hours or days separating the actual shooting of some shots in the same sequence and every aspect of each shot must match in order to maintain continuity. As each shot is completed, the CA logs any deviations from the script and minute details, such as with which hand an actor handled which prop. An instant camera is invaluable to a CA. After each shot the director, camera operator, and the audio operator will dictate comments to be added to the log. Each tape reel will have a separate log page, and often each reel may have more than one log page. The pages should be accurately labeled to match the labels on the tape reels. If copies are available, one goes in the box with the tape, one is kept with the assistant's files, and the third is delivered to the director.

150

RECORDER LOG PAGE

RECORDER LOG   DATE _____

LOCATION_____PRODUCTION _____

CAMERA / RECORDER _____ REEL _____

PRODUCER _____ DIRECTOR_____OPERATOR _____

COUNTER	TAKE	DESCRIPTION	REMARKS

151

Striking

Once the excitement of the actual production has evaporated and the actors, directors, and producers have disappeared, the last stage of the production process begins. It is just as important as any other stage, but it occurs when everyone is tired and let down after the tension of the shoot has eased and everyone is thinking about tomorrow.

As soon as the order to *strike* (a term borrowed from the theatre) has been given by the director, or production manager on a larger crew, all power is killed except for any work lights that are present. Then all other cables are disconnected to prevent crew members from tripping over them and pulling equipment and/or lighting instruments down. Each crew person has striking equipment responsibility. Cables are properly coiled and stored in their cases. Once equipment has been cleaned and returned to the proper cases, a check is made to be sure that all equipment has been packed and is ready to be loaded.

The strike should be as organized as the setup. The next use of the equipment may come the following day. Note any damaged equipment in writing and notify maintenance immediately. The location has to be restored to its original condition. You should repair any damage or report it to the owners in writing and negotiate a satisfactory compensation before you leave the site.

Equipment is then moved to the vehicle and loaded and returned to its storage locations. Each piece of equipment needs to be carefully checked off with the person responsible, whether it is the production manager or a leasing company. Take the same precautionary measures during striking as you did during the setup. Never leave equipment or the equipment vehicle unattended until all equipment has been secured.

The "fun" part of the production has now ended. It consumed the shortest period of time, and in many ways the least amount of effort, at least mental and aesthetic effort. Once you have worked several EFPs, you will appreciate the physical effort required for the production process.

STRIKE LIST

1. CAP CAMERA

2. TURN OFF ALL POWER SWITCHES EXCEPT WORK LIGHTS

3. DISMISS TALENT

4. DISCONNECT ALL CABLES, BOTH ENDS

5. LOWER ALL LIGHT STANDS, MOVE GENTLY OUT OF THE
WAY TO COOL

6. PICK UP AND PACK ALL PROPS, SET PIECES
LOAD SETS, LARGE SET PIECES

7. COIL CABLES PROPERLY, OVER-UNDER,
NOT AROUND ELBOW.

8. WIPE DOWN CABLES AND SECURELY FASTEN ENDS.

9. REMOVE CAMERA FROM TRIPOD,
PACK IN CASE WITH ACCESSORIES
(TRIPOD PLATE, POWER PACK) THAT BELONG IN CASE.

10. PACK ALL CABLES, BATTERIES

11. PACK ALL GAFFER EQUIPMENT

12. IF COOL, DISMANTLE LAMP HEADS AND STANDS
THEN PACK

13. INVENTORY ALL EQUIPMENT CASES
AND LOOSE EQUIPMENT

14. MOVE EQUIPMENT TO VEHICLE
** **NEVER LEAVE ANY EQUIPMENT UNATTENDED** **

15. LOAD EQUIPMENT INTO VEHICLE

Postproduction

The Editing Function

As the final stage of the video production process, postproduction affords the last opportunity to reach the goal originally set by the client. Regardless of the saying, "Fix it in post," not all errors in judgment, miscalculations, and poor production techniques can be corrected in postproduction. If the material is not available, or is technically deficient, there may not be any means of replacing it or rectifying the problems created in preproduction and/or production.

Most editors feel the truly creative portion of video production takes place in the editing room, and many directors and producers will agree. Video editing is a function that requires a combination of technical knowledge and skill, a great deal of aesthetic knowledge and sense, and unlimited patience.

The technical factors depend on the capabilities of the equipment available for the edit session. A wide range of editing equipment is available and the capabilities are being expanded daily. A good editor knows the limits of the equipment and has the ability to use the equipment to these limits without creating technical problems. The aesthetic factors call on a knowledge of psychology, art, music, theatre, and the rest of the performing arts. Editing is often a long and tedious process that stretches even the most patient persons to their limit.

The Editing System

The equipment used to edit videotape ranges from two videotape decks connected for dubbing to the most complex, computer-controlled, all-digital, non-linear systems. A beginning editor needs to know only the processes used in *control track (CT)* and *simple time code (TC)* editing.

In all editing suites there are at least three pieces of equipment: a controller, a source deck, and a record deck. More complex suites may use more than one source deck with *time base correctors (TBC)*, a video switcher, character and graphic generators, and an audio control board with a complement of audio sources.

Audio Sources

An audio control board is not an absolute requirement for a simple editing suite, but some means of setting audio levels should be included in the system, even if it is as simple as access to the audio controls on the tape decks. A more satisfactory system includes an audio board that feeds the outputs of both the audio tracks from each of the source decks plus audio tape decks, turntable, CD player, and microphone outputs through the board. This setup allows you to mix more than one audio source and control the levels and the equalization of the audio if the board is so designed.

Editing System Components

Controller

The *controller* is a specialized computer designed to perform three functions: controlling the playback functions of the source deck, controlling the play and record functions of the record deck, and storing this information. Controllers have a time read-out that indicates the position of each of the tapes in each of the decks. This time indicator on a control track system merely counts the control track pulses as they pass by a pick-up head. In a time code system, the indicator reads the exact position of the tape since the time code address is recorded directly onto the tape.

A controller utilizes either a knob or joy stick as a method of shuttling the tapes back and forth. A single control may be assigned to an individual machine as needed, or there may be shuttle controls for each machine in the system. The standard "play," "record," "fast forward," "rewind," and "stop" buttons for each machine also appear on the controller. In addition, a set of controls specifically designed for editing functions includes a method of choosing between assemble or insert editing; switches to choose recording of either or both audio tracks and/or the video track in the insert editing mode; a method of indicating the entry and exit edit points on the source machine(s) and recorder; and, depending on the editor, switches that allow previewing an edit without recording it, double-checking the entry and exit points, and reviewing the edit after it has been recorded.

Video Sources

The source deck, also called the *player*, and the recorder deck, sometimes known as the *editor*, are special videotape decks with additional circuits allowing the machines to be locked together in sync. The controls on the decks are the same as on any tape deck, but there are ports for connecting cables to the controller that are not present on a standard tape deck.

If the controller can handle more than one source deck, then a TBC for each source deck must be used to lock the recorders in sync so that a switcher may be used to record transitions other than cuts. Without TBCs and a switcher, cuts are the only transition possible. If character and/or graphic generators and a camera are to be included as additional sources, they may be used through a switcher as long as they are gen-locked to the system. Gen-locking is the process of tying all of the synchronous signals of the tape decks to the same time reference so shots may be freely combined through a switcher without causing the picture to lose sync and roll uncontrollably.

A/B ROLL
COMPLEX EDITING EQUIPMENT

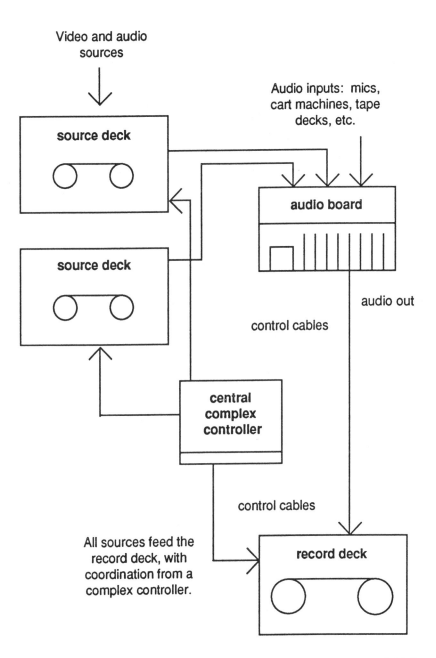

Video and audio sources

source deck

Audio inputs: mics, cart machines, tape decks, etc.

audio board

source deck

audio out

control cables

central complex controller

control cables

All sources feed the record deck, with coordination from a complex controller.

record deck

Editing Methods: Technical

Two types of technical edits can be made on videotape: an assemble edit or an insert edit.

Assemble Edit

An *assemble edit* records the video track, both audio tracks, and the control track simultaneously. This offers a quick and simple method of editing one shot after another, but it prevents you from editing the video separately from either of the audio tracks or any combination of the three.

Insert Edit

An *insert edit*, on the other hand, allows you to freely edit any of the three tracks separately, together, or in any combination. In order to achieve an insert edit though, a continuous series of the control track pulses must be recorded first. This process is called *laying down control track, black burst*, or *color bars*. In order to lay down a continuous series of CT, a complete video signal (no audio signal is needed) must be recorded on the tape.

One method, black burst, involves recording a black level signal from a signal generator or a switcher, or the signal from a capped camera. Another method is to record a color bars signal from a generator, switcher, or from a camera generating a color bars output. The signal must be continuous if the editing is to be accomplished on a CT editor. If the editing is on a time code editor, a time code signal is recorded either in the vertical interval portion of the video signal (VITC), a special time code track, or on an unused audio track at the same time as the black burst or color bars.

The choice of whether to record black or color bars on the video track depends on the final use of the tape. For master tapes that probably will not be duplicated, such as news stories, black is usually laid down. If a slight error is made in an edit that leaves a one- or two-frame gap between edits, the black will not be readily visible when the original master is played. On the other hand, if several generations of dubs are to be made with a frame or two of black, it may show as a flash or picture roll. When color bars are used, any gap between shots is easily seen at the time the tape is edited or previewed before dubs are made. Most professional postproduction facilities use color bars when laying down time code or control track.

Once black or color bar signals have been laid down, a professional editor seldom finds any need to edit other than in insert mode. If control track or sync pulses are accidentally erased or damaged, an assemble edit will be necessary to restore the continuity of both pulses, but the edit will have to continue beyond the length of the finished production or additional assemble edits will have to be made.

EDITING TRACK ARRANGEMENTS

Assemble Edit
Edited Shot

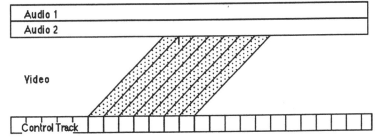

| Audio 1 | |
| Audio 2 | |

Video

Control Track

Simultaneous recording of both audio, video, and control track.
CANNOT record tracks separately.
Does not sync with prerecorded material at end of edit.

Insert Edit

Edited Shot

| Audio 1 | |
| Audio 2 | |

Video

Control Track

May record audio1, audio 2, or video tracks or any combination
of those three tracks.
DOES NOT re-record prerecorded control track.
Makes seamless edits and exits regardless of track choices.

Editing Operating Methods

Each studio, facility, or station will have a standard operating procedure (SOP) that designates exactly the format to be used in laying down black burst, color bars, tone, slate, and labeling of reels, cassettes, and boxes. The following is a compilation of SOP used that demonstrates the purposes of each segment of the operation.

You should shuttle a new tape in fast forward beyond the length of the anticipated edited master. Then rewind the tape to the beginning and reset the timer or time code reader to determine the beginning of the tape. Except for recording bars or black burst, no usable programming material should be recorded at the very beginning of a reel or cassette. Next, run the tape for 30 seconds to 1 minute to make certain that the tape stock is beyond any dirt that might have been picked up or any damaged tape that sometimes occurs at the start of a tape cassette or reel.

Lay down 30 seconds to 1 minute of tone with bars as video. If these two test signals are not set at the exact levels that will be used in the recording, they will be useless. These test signals are used by the technician preparing to play the tape back to set the play-back levels and adjust for *tracking*, *skew*, and other electronic adjustments. Following the tone and bars, record 10 seconds or so of a slate that specifies the title, length, client, date of recording, and, if a dub, which generation. Next, record a countdown with descending numbers from ten down to two, followed by a minimum of 2 seconds of clean black and then silence before the beginning of the first audio and video of the first shot of the edited production.

At the end of the production, at least 10 seconds of clean black and silence also need to be recorded. These periods of clean black and silence furnish a guard band of neutral signals in case there are errors in switching during a playback or to provide a logical space for dubbing.

MASTER TAPE SIGNALS

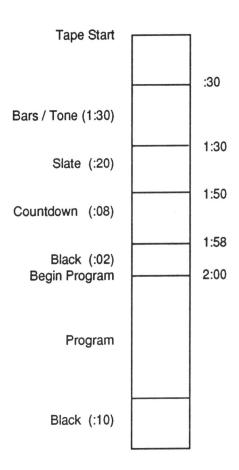

Master tapes for duplication and video disc masters require special signals for precise dubs. Check with duplication facility for their specifications.

Creating the Edit Decision List: Linear vs Nonlinear Editing

At this point a discussion of the difference between linear and nonlinear editing is appropriate. Until recently, videotape could only be edited in a linear manner; that is, each shot was added to the preceding. Changes could be made in either audio or video in already edited sequences as long as the overall length was not shortened or lengthened. Unlike film, which is edited in a nonlinear manner, a shot could be cut out or added at any point simply by splicing in a new shot or by cutting out an unwanted shot and resplicing at the removed shot in the film. Video editing does not involve physically cutting and splicing, so if a shot must be shortened or lengthened, all shots after the changed shot must be re-edited.

In a nonlinear video editing method, all of the shots are dubbed onto either a multitude of tape or disc players or onto a rapid access computer format. Instead of actually editing the tape, a non-linear system records the edit positions by the time code of each shot on a computer disk. The exact position of each shot on each reel of the raw footage is listed in order on an *Edit Decision List (EDL)*.

The EDL lists the shot number (from the script); the reel number; and the location on the reel in hours, minutes, seconds, and frames. This address number is visible on the screen if a time code has been recorded on the raw footage and can be seen on the timer if it is a control track editor.

The computer then can show you how the piece would look if edited together. Any changes you need to make are made in the EDL in the computer rather than on a tape deck. When the EDL is completed and approved, then the computer will control the playback machines, assembling the production according to the final EDL.

EDIT DECISION LIST

PRODUCTION ———————————————— PAGE ————————

PRODUCER ————————— EDITOR ——————————— DATE ————————

EDIT #	REEL	DESCRIPTION	VIDEO IN/OUT		AUDIO IN/OUT	

Editing Steps

Regardless of the level or complexity of the equipment used, the editing process consists of four basic steps: previewing the raw footage, physically preparing the master reel, laying down shots, and recording and marking the final production.

Assuming that you, as the editor, were not present during the shooting of the tape and that accurate logs were kept, your first action is to review all of the raw footage. Then you follow the logs and the script to begin to assimilate the material and reach an understanding on how the director interpreted the script with the shots recorded on the tape. If accurate logs were not kept during shooting, then you must carefully preview the tape and write a set of logs. If you were on the set at the time of shooting, the previewing process could be completed rapidly because you already would be familiar with the footage shot. While previewing the raw footage, you may create a rough EDL.

Off-line and On-line Editing
In order to avoid previewing, searching, and arriving at preliminary decisions in an expensive postproduction facility, dubs are made of the raw footage on a less expensive format with matching time code numbers: VHS if shot on U-matic, U-matic if shot on Betacam or M-II, and possibly professional 1/2 inch if shot on 1 inch or a digital format. This dub stock is then used to make a preliminary edited master. This process is called *off-line editing* because it utilizes a less expensive facility.

Once the off-line edit has been completed, the EDL, either hand-written or computerized by the off-line controller, and the original raw footage are taken to a fully equipped editing suite to create the on-line edited master. If the EDL is computer generated, the list is entered into the on-line computer, the tapes are cued up on a series of playback machines, and the computer then proceeds to make all of the edits, including transitions, special effects, and split edits.

If the off-line EDL was carefully made, then the on-line master can be edited automatically in a very short time, saving time and money. If minor changes need to be made after previewing the final master, the changes can be entered into the computer and that section will then be reedited.

If the on-line is not computerized, then the off-line EDL will act as a guide for quickly locating manually each shot on each reel in the order needed to assemble the final production. Although less efficient than the computerized method, the manual system still saves time and money in expensive on-line editing facilities.

EDIT DECISION LIST PROCESS

1. CHECK LABELS ON RAW FOOTAGE FROM SHOOT

2. RECORD TIME CODE ON VITC ,
    EXTRA AUDIO TRACK,
    OR SPECIAL TC TRACK IF NOT CODED
    WHEN RECORDED.

3. DUB RAW FOOTAGE AND TIME CODE
    TO OFF-LINE STOCK

4. PREVIEW AND LOG (OR CHECK LOGS)
    OF ALL FOOTAGE

5. EDIT OFF-LINE VERSION NOTING ALL
    EDIT POINTS (REEL NUMBER,
    EDIT NUMBER, ENTRY, EXIT POINTS,
    TRANSITION, AUDIO EDITS, AND
    SPECIAL EFFECTS) ON COMPUTER DISC,
    TAPE, OR MANUALLY

6. SEND ORIGINAL TAPE, OFF-LINE MASTER,
    AND EDL TO ON-LINE FACILITY.

7. FOOTAGE WILL BE CUED ON MULTIPLE
    PLAY-BACK DECKS AND COMPUTER
    WILL CONTROL ALL EDITING
    INSTRUCTIONS AS INDICATED ON
    THE EDL.

Creative Editing Methods

As in any creative, artistic field, there is an infinite number of methods of assembling a creative work. As a starting point professionals consider three basic methods of assembling a videotape.

In the first method, you lay down a master wide shot that covers in one take the entire sequence. Then you add individual CUs: cut-ins, cut-aways, and cover shots, as well as medium shots and reversals at appropriate times in the tape. Then, music and sound effects or voice-over narrations may be added to fit the edited video. The advantage of this method is that the master shot determines the length of the sequence. For commercials and some news stories, the overall length must not exceed a specific time period. An interview can be edited in this manner, as can a demonstration or a musical sequence. The disadvantage is that you are tied to the master shot. If a CU does not match the length of the same line or action in the master shot, the CU cannot be used because continuity will be lost.

A second method requires you to edit one shot after another in sequence. You add cover shots to smooth transitions and avoid jump cuts. This method requires an editor with considerable skill and knowledge of the production and the available raw footage. You may add music and sound effects either as the editing progresses or after all of the video has been assembled.

In the third method, you prerecord the audio and lay down the main audio track first. In a narration-based production, the narration is the main audio track. Once it is laid down, you then record shots matching the narration. Music and sound effects may be added last. An alternative to this method, often used with music videos, is when the music is laid down first, and then shots of the musician lip syncing to the music are matched to the music. Additional dramatic or illustrative shots are added at appropriate times during the musical number. You may mix sound effects with the music before or after the audio track is laid down or utilize the second audio track.

In reality, most editors use a combination of all three methods, depending on the needs of the production during that particular sequence. If the master tape is to be duplicated, then you must write specific and precise instructions according to the recommendations of the International Teleproduction Society (ITS).

Your final duties as an editor include properly labeling all of the master and raw footage tape stock, both the tape as well as the boxes in which they are stored. All paper records—shooting and editing logs, director's/producer's instructions, and bookkeeping forms and records required by the accounting department—must be filled out and/or properly filed. Your work as an editor ends as it began, dealing with a pile of paperwork in order to better perform your job.

EDITING METHODS

Master shot and CU's

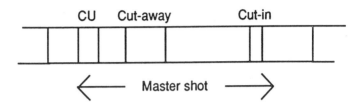

CU   Cut-away   Cut-in

⟵   Master shot   ⟶

Shot Sequencing

	shot 1	shot 2	shot 3	shot 4	shot 5	shot 6	

Master video to audio

audio recorded first

	# 1	# 2	# 3	# 4	# 5	# 6	# 7	

shots edited to match audio

Conclusion

As it is now obvious from the reading of this text, there is as much paperwork in media production as there is of any other single activity. The actual shooting of the production constitutes a minimum amount of the total time, though usually a maximum of the total physical effort, that goes into the production.

The critical stages occur during the preproduction and editing processes. If a production is not clearly and carefully planned before shooting starts, no amount of creative or physical effort will save the production. By the same token, if the shooting is not specifically planned to be edited, no amount of effort in the editing suite will salvage the production.

My best advice is to plan for the worst and shoot for the best.

Further Reading

Alkin, Glyn. *Sound techniques for Video and TV.* 2nd ed. Stoneham, MA: Focal Press, 1989.

Amyes, Tim. *The Technique of Audio Post Production in Video and Film.* Stoneham, MA: Focal Press, 1990.

Anderson, Gary. *Electronic Post-Production: The Film to Video Guide.* White Plains, NY: Knowledge Industry Publications, Inc., 1986.

———. *Video Editing and Post Production: A Professional Guide.* 2nd ed. White Plains, NY: Knowledge Industry Publications, Inc. 1988.

Armer, Alan A. *Directing Television and Film.* 2nd ed. Belmont, CA: Wadsworth Publishing Co., 1990.

Bernard, Robert. *Practical Videography.* Stoneham, MA: Focal Press, 1990.

Borwick, John. *Microphones: Technology and Techniques.* Stoneham, MA: Focal Press, 1990.

Browne, Steven E. *Videotape Editing: A Postproduction Primer,* 2nd ed. Stoneham, MA: Focal Press, Inc., 1993.

Cipher Digital Time Code Handbook. Frederick, MD: Cipher Digital, Inc., 1987.

Dancyger, Ken. *Broadcast Writing: Drama, Comedies, and Documentaries.* Stoneham, MA: Focal Press, 1991.

DiZazzo, Ray. *Corporate Television: A Producer's Handbook.* Stoneham, MA: Focal Press, 1990.

Fuller, Barry J., Steve, Kanaba, and Janyce Brisch-Kanaba. *Single-camera Video Production: Techniques, Equipment, and Resources for Producing Quality Video Programs.* Englewood Cliffs, NJ: Prentice-Hall, Inc., 1982.

Hartwig, Robert L. *Basic TV Technology.* Stoneham, MA: Focal Press, 1990.

Hausman, Carl. *Institutional Video: Planning, Budgeting, Production and Evaluation.* Belmont, CA: Wadsworth Publishing Co., 1991.

Katz, Steven D. *Film Directing Shot by Shot: Visualizing from Concept to Screen.* Stoneham, MA: Focal Press, 1991.

LeTourneau, Tom. *Lighting Techniques for Video Production: The Art of Casting Shadows.* White Plains, NY: Knowledge Industry Publications, Inc., 1987.

Mathias, Harry, and Richard Patterson. *Electronic Cinematography: Achieving Photographic Control over the Video Image.* Belmont, CA: Wadsworth Publishing Co., 1985.

Medoff, Norman J., and Tom Tanquary. *Portable Video ENG and EFP.* White Plains, NY: Knowledge Industry Publications, Inc., 1986.

Miller, Pat P. *Script Supervising and Film Continuity.* 2nd ed. Stoneham, MA: Focal Press, Inc. 1990.

Millerson, Gerald. *The Technique of Lighting for Television and Films.* Stoneham, MA: Focal Press, 1991.

———. *The Technique of Television Production.* 12th ed. Stoneham, MA: Focal Press, Inc., 1990.

———. *Television Scenic Design Handbook.* Stoneham, MA: Focal Press, 1989.

———. *Video Production Handbook.* Stoneham, MA: Focal Press, Inc., 1987.

Morley, John. *Scriptwriting for High-Impact Video.* Belmont, CA: Wadsworth Publishing Co., 1992.

Patterson, Richard, and Dana White, eds. *Electronic Production Techniques.* Los Angeles: American Cinematographer, 1983.

Paulson, C. Robert. *BM/E's ENG/EFP/EPP Handbook.* New York: Broadband Information Services, Inc., 1981.

Rabiger, Michael. *Directing the Documentary.* Stoneham, MA: Focal Press, 1987.

Robinson, J. F., and P. H. Beards. *Using Videotape.* 2nd ed. Stoneham, MA: Focal Press, Inc., 1981.

Robinson, J. F., and Stephen Lowe. *Videotape Recording.* Stoneham, MA: Focal Press, 1981.

Rosenthal, Alan. *Writing, Directing, and Producing Documentaries.* Carbondale, IL: Southern Illinois University Press, 1990.

Schihl, Robert J. *Single Camera Video: From Concept to Edited Master.* Stoneham, MA: Focal Press, Inc., 1989.

Schneider, Arthur. *Electronic Post-Production Terms and Concepts.* Stoneham, MA: Focal Press, 1990.

———. *Electronic Post-Production and Videotape Editing.* Stoneham, MA: Focal Press, 1989.

172

Shetter, Michael D. *Videotape Editing: A Guide to Communicating Pictures and Sound.* Elk Grove Village, IL: Swiderski Electronics, Inc., 1982.

Shook, Frederick. *Television Field Production and Reporting.* New York: Longman, Inc., 1989.

Whittaker, Ron. *Video Field Production.* Mountain View, CA: Mayfield Publishing Co., 1989.

Zettl, Herbert. *Sight-Sound-Motion.* 2nd ed. Belmont, CA: Wadsworth Publishing Co., 1990.

———. *Television Production Handbook.* 5th ed. Belmont, CA: Wadsworth Publishing Co., 1991.

173

Glossary

A/B ROLL Editing process using two separate rolls (cassettes or reels) of tape. Each cassette contains alternate shots of the sequence, thus enabling the editor to use transitions other than straight cuts between shots.

ADDITIVE COLORS The colors used in mixing light and upon which both film and video signals are based: red, blue, and green.

AMBIANT Prevailing environment; in audio, the background noise present at a location.

AMPLITUDE The instantaneous value of a signal; the electronic equivalent of level or loudness in audio.

ANALOG Electronic signal that is constantly varying in some proportion to either sound, light, or a radio frequency.

APERTURE (Iris) The size of the lens opening, measured in f-stops.

ASSEMBLE EDIT Sequential arranging of shots in a linear manner. May be accomplished on raw tape without previously recording a control track.

AUDIO The sound portion of the videotape. Frequencies within the normal hearing range of humans.

AURAL Having to do with sound or audio.

AUTOMATIC GAIN CONTROL (AGC) Circuit that maintains the audio or video level within a certain range. Prevents overdriving circuits, which causes distortion, but can increase signal to noise ratio.

AVAILABLE LIGHT Illumination existing at a location.

BACK LIGHT Light placed behind the subject, opposite the camera; usually mounted fairly high and controlled with barndoors to prevent light shining directly into the camera lens.

BARNDOOR Movable metal flaps attached to lighting fixtures to allow control over the area covered by the light from that lamp.

BARREL A cable adaptor designed to connect two cables ending in similar plugs.

BASS The low end of the audio spectrum.

BETACAM 1/2-inch professional videotape format developed by Sony specifically for use in a camcorder. Has replaced 3/4 U-matic as the predominate news gathering video format. Now upgraded to BetaSP.

BI-DIRECTIONAL Microphone that picks up sound from the front and back but rejects most sound from the sides. The pickup pattern appears in the shape of a figure eight.

BLACK BURST A composite video signal including sync and color signals, but the video level is at black, or minimum.

BLACK LEVEL The normal level for pedestal or video black in a video signal. See also **setup**.

BLEED Space beyond the critical or essential area that may be seen on some television receivers but not on others.

BLOOM The effect seen when a video signal exceeds the capabilities of the system: white areas bleed into darker areas.

BODY MIKE A microphone concealed or hung directly on the body of the performer, sometimes called a *lapel* or *lavalier* mike.

BOOM Movable arm from which a microphone or camera may be suspended to allow for movement to follow the action.

BNC A type of twist-lock video connector, now the most common for professional equipment.

BROAD A type of open-faced fill light, usually rectangular in shape.

BUBBLE Leveling device mounted on a tripod pan head consisting of a tube containing a liquid with a bubble of air trapped inside. Centering the bubble on a circle or cross-hair indicates that the pan head is level.

BURN A condition caused by exposing camera tubes to excessive light levels. An image is retained on the face of the tube that is the negative of the original subject.

"C" FORMAT One of three 1-inch helical videotape formats specified by the SMPTE. "C" has become the analog production standard for studios in the United States.

CAMCORDER Camera-recorder combination. Designed originally for news coverage, but now becoming popular for EFP and other field productions.

CARDIOID MIKE Specialized unidirectional microphone with a heart-shaped pickup pattern.

CASE, upper or lower style of letters. Upper-case letters are capital letters; lower-case letters are small letters.

176

CASSETTE Prepackaged container of either audio or videotape containing a specific length of tape stock, a feed reel, and a take-up reel. U-matic, Betacam, VHS, and M-II Systems all use incompatible video cassettes.

CHARACTER GENERATOR (CG) Computerized electronic typewriter designed to create titles or any other numeric or alphanumeric graphics for use in video.

CHARGE COUPLED DEVICE (CCD) A solid-state element designed to convert light to electronics; replaces the pickup tubes in video cameras.

CHIP Semiconductor integrated circuit. Depending on design, can replace tubes, resistors, and other electronic components. The most important development for EFP is the light-sensitive chip that replaces the camera tube.

CHROMINANCE The portion of the video signal controlling color.

CHIAROSCURO LIGHTING Lighting accomplished with high contrast areas and heavy shadows.

CINEMATOGRAPHER Its narrowest definition is the operator or supervisor of a motion-picture camera; over the years it has, to some, included the field of operating a video camera.

CLOSE UP (CU) Camera framing showing intimate detail. Often a tight head shot.

CLOSURE Psychological perceptual activity that fills in gaps in the visual field.

COLOR BARS Electronically generated pattern of precisely specified colors for use in standardizing the operation of video equipment.

COLOR TEMPERATURE See **Kelvin temperature**.

CONDENSER MIKE Transducer that converts sound waves by conductive principle. Requires a built-in amplifier and a power source. Also called *electrostatic* or *capacitor*.

CONTINUITY A depiction of continuous action.

CONTRAST RANGE Ability of a camera to distinguish between shades of reflected black and white light: TV, 30:1; film, 100:1; human eye 1000:1.

CONTROLLER A specialized computer designed to accurately maintain control over a series of videotape decks during the editing process.

CONTROL TRACK Synchronizing signal recorded onto a videotape to align the heads for proper playback.

COOKY See cukaloris.

COPY The words on a script.

COUNTER A meter designed to indicate either a position on a reel of tape

177

or the amount of tape already used. May be calibrated in revolutions, feet, meters, or time.

CRITICAL AREA (ESSENTIAL AREA) Space occupying approximately 80 percent of the center of the video frame. This area will be seen with relative surety by the majority of the television receivers viewing that particular program. The 10 percent border outside of the critical area may not be seen by many receivers.

CUE 1) Signal to start talking, moving, or whatever the script calls for. 2) To ready material to be played back or edited by running and stopping a tape, film, record, etc., at a specified spot.

CUKALORIS A pattern inserted into an ellipsoidal spotlight to throw a mottled design onto the background.

CUT (Take) 1)Cue to stop an action, etc. 2) an instantaneous change in picture or sound. "Cut" is considered a film term, "take," a video term, but they have become interchangeable.

CUT-IN Close-up shot of an image visible in the wider shot immediately preceding or following it.

CUT-AWAY Close-up shot of an image related to, but not visible in, the wider shot immediately preceding or following it.

CYCLE Time or distance between peaks of an alternating voltage. Measured in hertz.

DECK In media refers to a machine that plays and/or records audio or video signals.

DECIBEL (dB) Logarithmic unit of loudness. A dB is 1/10 of the original unit, the Bel.

DEPTH OF FIELD (DOF) The range of distances from the camera within which subjects remain in acceptable focus.

DIALOGUE Speech between performers, usually seen on camera.

DICHROIC Filters designed to reflect certain colors of light and pass others.

DIGITAL Binary-based, constant-amplitude signals varying in time. Provides signal recording without noise or distortion.

DIN (Deutsche Industrie Normen) The German standards organization. DIN usually refers to a type of plug/jack.

DIRECTOR Commands the creative aspects of a production. In the field, makes creative decisions; in the studio, calls the shots on live productions; and in the editing room, provides opinions.

DISSOLVE Transition of one image fading into and replacing another. If stopped at the midpoint, it is a superimposition. Also called *lap*.

DISTORTION An undesirable change in a signal.

178

DISTRIBUTION AMPLIFIER (DA) Electronic amplifier designed to feed one signal (audio, video, or pulses) to several different destinations.

DOLLY 1) Three- or four-wheeled device that serves as a movable camera mount. 2) Movement in toward a subject (dolly in) or back away from a subject (dolly out).

DOWN LINK Transmission path from a satellite to a ground station. Sometimes used to describe the ground station capable of receiving a satellite signal. See **up link**.

DUB 1) Copying a recorded signal from one medium to another. 2) Replacing or adding voice to a preexisting recording. Now called *Automatic Dialogue Replacement (ADR)*.

DYNAMIC MIKE Transducer designed to convert sound to electronics by using an electromagnetic coil attached to a lightweight diaphragm.

DYNAMIC RANGE Loudness range from softest to the loudest that can be reproduced by any system without creating distortion.

EDIT DECISION LIST (EDL) List of precise locations of edit points. May be generated manually or by computer.

EDITOR Tape or film specialist charged with assembling stories from footage and recordings to create the final production.

EIAJ (Electronic Industries Association of Japan) Standards setting organization of Japan. At one time referred to a specific 1/2-inch open-reel videotape system.

ELECTRONIC NEWS GATHERING (ENG) Process of researching, shooting, and editing materials to visually report on occurrences of interest utilizing video cameras and electronic editing specifically for newscasts.

EQUALIZATION Process of compensating for required changes in frequency, level, or phase of an audio or video signal.

EXTREME CLOSE (ECU or XCU) Tightest framing of a shot in a sequence. For example, just the eyes or hands of a subject.

EXTREME WIDE SHOT (EWS or XWS) Widest shot of a sequence. For example, an entire city block or football stadium.

EXTERIOR A setting or location outdoors.

"F" (see RF) A type of cable connector for a cable intended to carry a modulated signal or signals.

FACSIMILE (FAX) Transmission of information by optical/electronic system through telephone lines.

FACILITIES (FAX) Technical equipment, lights, cameras, microphones, etc.

FADE, IN OR OUT A gradual change in signal either from zero to maximum or maximum to zero. Either audio or video.

FEDERAL COMMUNICATION COMMISSION (FCC) Federal government agency charged with the supervision and regulation of all electronic communication media in this country.

FIELD One half of a complete television picture. 262.5 lines of the 525 NTSC system occurring once every 60th of a second. Two fields make a complete frame.

FILL LIGHT Soft, shadowless light used to reduce contrast and lighten shadow areas. Usually placed on the opposite side of the camera from the key light and low enough to remove harsh shadows.

FISHPOLE Handheld expandable mike boom.

FLAG An opaque piece of material hung between a light and subject or set to control light or throw a shadow.

FLASH FRAME An unwanted frame between two edited shots.

FLUORESCENT LIGHT Gas-filled tube that emits light when an electrical current ionizes the gas. It does not emit light of a specific Kelvin temperature, but is bluish green in color.

FLYING ERASE HEAD Erase head mounted on the rotating head mount of a helical recorder. Designed to allow precise editing of the video signal without loosing sync between shots.

FOCAL LENGTH Theoretical distance from the optical center of the lens to the focal plane. Determines, with the size of the image surface, the angle of view, depth of field, and image size.

FOCUS The ability of a lens to create the sharpest image of a subject.

FOLEY Named for Jack Foley, an early sound operator in film. A studio designed to create sounds in postproduction.

FOOT CANDLE Older measurement of illumination. Originally, the amount of light from 1 candle, falling on an area 1 foot square, 1 foot from the candle.

FORMAT, VIDEOTAPE Specifications of a specific type of videotape. There are approximately 18 different formats in common usage today.

FRAME 1) Complete video picture, made up of two 262.5 line interlaced scanned fields. There are 30 frames a second in the NTSC system. 2) The outline of the available area in which to compose a video picture. Today's NTSC standard is a frame 3 units high by 4 units wide.

FREQUENCY Number of complete cycles an electrical signal makes in one second. Measured in hertz, Hz.

FREQUENCY RESPONSE A measurement of a piece of equipment's ability to reproduce a signal of varying frequencies.

FRESNEL A spotlight equipped with a stepped lens that easily controls and concentrates light.

180

F–STOP   A measurement of the size of opening that allows light to pass through an iris or aperture.

GAFFER   Senior electrician on a crew.

GAIN   The amount of amplitude of an electronic signal. Usually measured in dB.

GENRE   A type of programming; i.e., western, comedy.

GIGAHERTZ   A measurement of frequency, 1 billion hertz.

GIRAFFE   Small mike boom mounted on a tripod on wheels usually designed for limited mike movement.

GOBO   1) In video, a set piece that allows a camera to shoot through it, such as a window. 2) In audio, a movable sound reflector board. 3) In film, a movable freestanding pattern cut-out similar to a cookie. 4) On stage, the equivalent of a cookie.

GRAPHICS GENERATOR   A digital unit designed to create and combine pictures with type. Sometimes called a *paint box.*

GRAY SCALE   Multiple-step intensity scale for the evaluation of a picture. Generally, there are 10 steps between television white and television black.

GRIP   A stagehand, a crew person who moves sets, props, dollies. The head stagehand is the **key grip.**

GUN   A part of a picture and a camera tube that shoots a stream of electronics at the face plate of the tube.

HEAD   A pan head supports the camera and is designed to allow both horizontal and vertical movement of the camera.

HELICAL   Videotape with multiple recording heads that records information in long slanting tracks; each track records one field of information.

HERTZ (Hz)   Measurement of frequency. Number of complete cycles completed in 1 second.

HI–8   Semiprofessional 8mm videotape format developed by Sony for the "prosumer" market.

HIGH DEFINITION TELEVISION (HDTV)   One of several subcategories of Advanced TV (ATV). Attempt at creating a video system nearly equal to 35mm film in resolution and aspect ratio.

HI HAT   A minimal platform designed to mount a pan head allowing for shots close to the ground or to mount the camera on a car, boat, or airplane.

IMAGE ORTHICON (I-O)   An early video camera tube. The development of the I-O opened the way for reasonably mobile studio and remote cameras.

181

IMPEDANCE Apparent AC resistance to current flowing in a circuit. Measured in Ohms.

INCANDESCENT LIGHT Inert-gas-filled electric lamp emitting light and heat from a glowing filament. A typical lamp is the tungsten-halogen lamp used in most production instruments.

INCIDENT LIGHT Illumination from a light source. Measured in foot candles or Lux by pointing the light meter at the light source.

INPUT Signal entering a system or an electrical unit.

INSERT EDIT Assembling a videotape production by adding video and audio signals to tape stock that already has had control track recorded on it. Insert edits also can be made over existing edited tape.

INTERIOR Setting or location inside of a building or structure.

INTERLACE SCANNING The method of combining two fields of scan lines into one frame.

INTRO Abbreviation for introduction.

INVERSE SQUARE LAW A mathematical analysis of changes in alternating energy. The amount of energy is inversely proportionate to the change in distance. The formula is easily applied to calculating lighting and audio levels.

IRIS See **aperture**.

JARGON Terminology and slang of a particular field.

JUMP CUT Any one of several types of poor edits that either break continuity or may be disturbing to the audience.

KELVIN TEMPERATURE Measurement of the relative color of light. Indicated as degrees Kelvin; the higher the temperature, the bluer the light, the lower the temperature, the redder the light.

KEY LIGHT Apparent main source of light. Usually from one bright light above and to one side of the camera.

KICKER A light focused from the side on the subject or on a particular section of the set.

KILOHERTZ A measurement of alternating energy; 1000 hertz.

LAG That characteristic of a camera tube in which a picture trails its own images as the camera moves. Lag increases with the age of the tube.

LAVALIER (Lav) Microphone worn around the neck. Also sometimes called a **LAPEL** mic when clipped to a tie or front of the clothing.

LENS Glass or plastic designed to focus and concentrate light on a surface to form an image.

LENS CAP Opaque covering to slip over the end of a lens to protect the surface from damage and to protect the image device from excessive light.

182

LEVEL Relative amplitude or intensity. Used to indicate light, audio, video, and other electronic signals.

LIGHT EMITTING DIODE (LED) A solid-state component that emits light when a small voltage is applied. Useful as a level or operating condition indicator.

LIGHT METER (Exposure meter) Instrument used to measure the intensity of light. May be calculated in foot candles, Lux, or f-stops.

LINE LEVEL Signal amplified enough to feed down a line without fear of degradation. A microphone level is lower than line level; speaker level is higher.

LOCATION Area or site of a production. Usually refers to sites away from studios.

LOG Listing of shots as they are recorded on tape.

LONGITUDINAL Lengthwise, refers in media to the method of recording audio and control track signals.

LOOPING The process of rerecording audio during postproduction. Also now called *Automatic Dialogue Replacement (ADR)*.

LOUDNESS Perceived intensity of audio. Depends on the intensity and saturation of the sound, as well as the sensitivity of the listener to a range of frequencies.

LUMINANCE The brightness component of a video signal.

LUX European measurement of light intensity. There are approximately 10 Lux to 1 foot candle.

MASTER SHOT Extended wide shot establishing the scene and often running the entire length of the sequence. Intended to be broken down in the editing process.

MEDIUM CLOSE UP (MCU) Relative average framing for a shot. Often framed from the waist up.

MEDIUM SHOT (MS) Wider than an MCU, often framed head to toe.

M FORMAT (M–II, Recam) Panasonic's professional 1/2-inch format. Originally sold by RCA as Recam, then upgraded to M–II. Now competing with Sony's BetacamSP.

MICROWAVE High-frequency carrier for both audio and video signals. Operates only on a line-of-sight path.

MINI-PLUG (1/8-inch) Audio connector designed for small equipment. Scaled down version of 1/4-inch phone plug.

MIXER A piece of electronic equipment designed to combine several signals. Usually refers to an audio board or console.

MODULATOR An electronic component designed to impress one signal on another, usually of a higher frequency.

183

MONITOR 1) To listen to or watch audio or videotapes or off-air programs. 2) Device used to view video signals. Much like a TV receiver, but is usually much higher quality and generally does not have an RF section for off-the-air monitoring.

MORGUE Library, reference files, storage for used scripts, tapes, maps, and other reference material.

MOS 1) Metal oxide semiconductor. A type of camera chip that replaces the camera tube. 2) A film term indicating a shot was recorded silent, or as the early German film directors said, "Mit out sound."

NAT SOUND Ambient sound that exists on location recorded as a story happens. Often used as background for a VO. Sometimes called *wild sound.*

NEUTRAL DENSITY A type of filter that decreases light passage without changing the color value of the light.

NOISE Any undesirable additions to a signal.

NOTAN A lighting style similar to Japanese watercolors: high key, few shadows, evenly lit.

NTSC (National Television Standards Committee) 1) The organization charged with setting television standard in the United States in the early days of television. 2) The television standard now in use in North America, much of South America, and Japan.

OFF-LINE Using the lowest quality and cost editing system suitable for a particular project.

OMNIDIRECTIONAL Microphone pickup pattern that covers 360 degrees around the mike.

ON-LINE Using the highest quality and cost editing system suitable for a particular project.

OPERATOR Person whose main responsibility is to operate equipment, as contrasted with technicians, whose main responsibility it is to install, repair, and maintain equipment, and engineers, whose main responsibility it is to research, design, and construct equipment.

OPTICS-OPTICAL Having to do with lenses or other light-carrying components of a video or film system.

OSCILLOSCOPE Test equipment used to visualize a time factor system such as a video signal. Shows a technician what the picture looks like electronically. Also may be used to analyze audio or other signals.

OUTPUT Signal leaving a system or electrical unit.

PAN Horizontal movement of a camera, short for *panorama.*

PAN HEAD Mechanism designed to firmly hold a camera on the top of a tripod, pedestal, or boom while allowing for smooth, easily controlled movement of the camera horizontally (pan) and vertically (tilt). May be mechanical, fluid, or counterbalanced.

PARABOLIC MIKE   Focused, concave, reflective, bowl-shaped surface with a mike mounted at the point of focus. Used to pick up specific sounds at a distance. Commonly used during sporting events.

PEDESTAL   1) Electronic calibration between blanking and black level. 2) Hydraulic, compressed air, or counterbalanced studio camera mount. Designed to permit the camera to be raised straight up or down effortlessly and smoothly.

PERAMBULATOR   A large, wheeled, platform-mounted boom that a mike boom operator rides. Capable of swinging a mike over a large area.

PHANTOM POWER   48 volts required by condenser mike preamplifiers located in the mike. If the mike does not carry its own battery power, may be supplied through the mike line by the mixer or recorder.

PHASE   The relationship of two signals differing in time but on a common path.

PHASE ALTERNATIVE LINE (PAL)   A television system developed in England using 625 lines and 50 frames rather than the 525–60 system of NTSC. Used in many countries around the world.

PHOTOGRAPHER   Originally, a person taking still photographs. In some markets term was applied to news cinematographers and even today sometimes is applied to videographers.

PLOSIVE SOUNDS   Sounds made by the human voice that tend to "pop" a microphone. Sounds beginning with the letters "p" and "b" among others.

PLOT   A scale drawing of the location of a shoot.

POINT OF VIEW (POV)   A camera angle giving the impression of the view of someone in the scene.

PREAMPLIFIER (Preamp)   Electronic circuit designed to amplify weak signal to usable level without introducing noice or distortion.

PRIME LENS   A fixed focal length lens.

PRISM   A glass or plastic block shaped to transmit or reflect light into different paths.

PRODUCER   Person in charge of a specific program.

PROMPTER   Device used to provide the talent with the copy as they sit on camera. Can be copy handheld beside the camera or a signal fed to a monitor mounted with mirrors to project the copy in front of the camera lens so the anchor can look directly into the camera. This signal may be coming from a black-and-white camera shooting pages of the script or from a signal fed directly from a computer.

185

PROPOSAL A concise summary of a project intended as a sales tool to accurately describe a production and to sell a sponsor on funding.

PROSUMER A category of producer and equipment that falls below that of a professional but at a higher quality than a consumer.

PUBLIC ADDRESS (PA) Sound reinforcing system designed to feed sound to an audience assembled in a large room.

QUADRAPLEX (Quad) First practical professional videotape format. Used 2-inch tape pulled across four heads to achieve a high quality signal. No longer manufactured.

QUARTER-INCH PLUG (Phone) Audio connector used for many years for high-impedance signals. Still used in some consumer equipment and patch panels.

RASTER The complete sequence of lines that make up the field of lines creating a video picture.

RCA The American corporation that promoted the NTSC video system, the developer of many early television inventions, and the original owner of NBC radio and television.

RCA PLUG (Phono) Audio and video connector designed originally for use only with the RCA 45 rpm record player. Now used as consumer audio and video connector. Some professional equipment uses this plug for line level audio. Not to be confused with the phone (1/4-inch plug).

REFLECTED LIGHT Illumination entering a lens reflected from an object. Measured with a reflected light meter pointing at the object from the camera.

REGISTRATION The alignment of either electronic or physical components of a system. Especially important in tube cameras.

RELEASE 1) Legal document allowing the videographer to use the image and/or voice of a subject. 2) Public relations copy.

RESOLUTION Ability of a system to reproduce fine detail. In video there are limits imposed by the NTSC video system.

RF Abbreviation for *radio frequency.* 1) Those frequencies above the aural frequencies. 2) A type of plug attached to a cable designed to carry a modulated signal.

RIBBON MIKE A transducer utilizing a thin gold or silver corrugated ribbon suspended between the poles of a magnet to create an electrical output.

SATELLITE Geostationary orbiting space platform with transponders to pick up signals from the Earth and retransmit the signals back down to Earth in a pattern, called a *footprint,* that covers a large area of the Earth.

186

SATURATION   Intensity of a signal, either audio or video, but especially used as the third of three characteristics of a color video signal.

SCENE   A series of related shots, usually in the same time and location.

SCENE SCRIPT   A full script without individual shots indicated.

SCRIM   A metalic or fabric filter placed over a lighting instrument to diffuse and soften the light.

SCRIPT   Complete manuscript of all audio copy and video instructions of a program.

SET UP   Assemble equipment and people in preparation for rehearsing a production.

SET-UP   Same as pedestal and black level; electronic calibration between blanking and black level.

SEQUENCE   Individual shots edited into scenes, and individual scenes edited together to make a story.

SEQUENTIAL COLOUR AVEC MEMOIRE (SECAM)   The color television system developed by the French and in use in many countries around the world.

SHOOTING SCRIPT   A script complete in all details, including specific shot descriptions.

SHOT   One continuous roll of the recorder. The smallest unit of a script.

SHOTGUN   Ultra-unidirectional microphone designed to pick up sound at a distance by excluding unwanted sound from the sides of the mike.

SHOT SHEET   A listing of all shots in the order they are to be made, regardless of their order in the script.

SHUTTLE   Movement of videotape back and forth while searching for edit points. Usually done at speeds faster or slower than real time.

SIGNAL-TO-NOISE RATIO (S/N Ratio)   The mathematical ratio between the noise level in a signal to the program level. The higher the ratio, the better the signal.

SITE SURVEY   A detailed listing of all the information needed to shoot on location at a certain site.

SKEW   Tension adjustment during videotape playback. Visible as a "bending" at the extreme top of the picture.

SLATE   Several frames identifying the shot, tape reel number, or other logging information. Usually recorded at the beginning of the tape.

SOFTLIGHT   A large light fixture that emits a well-diffused light over a broad area.

SOP (Standard Operating Procedure)   Predetermined methods of accomplishing tasks. Often set by corporate or upper management policy.

SPOT METER A light meter designed to read a very small area of reflected light.

SPLITTER BOX Device used to feed an input signal to more than one output. Commonly used at news conferences to avoid a jumble of microphones by splitting the feed from one mike to all those covering the event.

STORYBOARD A series of drawings indicating each shot and accompanying audio in a production.

SUPERIMPOSITIONS (Supers) Two or more simultaneously fed video signals, stopping a dissolve at the halfway point.

SWISH PAN A rapid horizontal movement of the camera while recording. May be used as a transition device.

SWITCHER 1) In multicamera or postproduction, a device used to change video sources feeding the recording tape deck. 2) The person operating the video switcher.

SYNCHRONOUS (Sync) Signals locked in proper alignment with each other; sound and picture locked together, all the various video signals in their proper relationship to each other.

TENT An opaque sheet of material suspended over a subject to diffuse and soften the light.

TIME BASE CORRECTOR (TBC) Electronic device used to lock together signals with dissimilar sync. Also may be used to correct for phase, level, and pedestal errors in original recordings.

TIME CODE Time based address recorded on videotape to allow for precise editing. SMPTE time code is one most universally used at present.

TILT The vertical movement of a camera on a pan head.

TRACKING 1) Aligning playback heads on a VCR with the original pattern of video recorded on tape. 2) Movement of a camera to the left or right, usually while mounted on a set of tracks for maximum smoothness and control.

TRANSDUCER Any device used to convert any form of energy to another form: a camera transduces light to video; a microphone transduces sound to electronics; a speaker transduces electronics to sound.

TRANSFORMER Magnetic voltage- or impedance-changing device.

TREATMENT A narrative description of a production. It should read more like a novel than a script since it is intended for a nonmedia person.

TREBLE High frequencies of the audio band.

TRIPOD Three-legged portable camera support.

TUNGSTEN LIGHT Relatively efficient gas-filled light source of approximately 3200°K temperature.

UHF (Ultra High Frequency)   1) Frequency band for television broadcasting channels 14–69. 2) An older, large, threaded type of video connector.

U-MATIC   3/4-inch videotape format created by Sony in the early 1970s that revolutionized video news gathering. Has been upgraded by a compatible U-maticSP format.

UNIDIRECTIONAL   Microphone pickup pattern from a single direction. Comes in a variety of degrees of pickup angle, from cardioid to super unidirectional (shotgun).

UP LINK   Transmission path from an Earth-based station up to a satellite. Sometimes used to describe the ground station capable of sending a satellite signal. See **DOWN LINK.**

VARIABLE FOCAL LENGTH LENS (Zoom)   A lens that can have its focal length changed while in use.

VECTORSCOPE   Electronic test equipment designed to show the color aspects of the video signal.

VERTICAL INTERVAL TIME CODE (VITC)   Time address recorded within the vertical interval blanking instead of on a separate linear track.

VHS, S-VHS   JVC-developed consumer VCR system, VHS stands for Video Home System. "S" in S-VHS stands for "separate" since it is a semicompatible component recording system, rather than a composite system.

VIDEO   1) Picture portion of an electronic visual system. 2) All-inclusive term for electronic visual reproduction systems; includes television, cablevision, corporate media, and video recording.

VIDEOGRAPHER   The proper term for the operator of a video camera.

VIDICON   A type of video camera tube that replaced the Image Orthicon. It is lighter, smaller, and more durable and provides higher resolution.

VIEWFINDER   The miniature video monitor mounted on the camera so the operator can see what is framed by the camera.

VISUAL   The video portion of the program.

VOICE OVER (VO)   Story that uses continuous visuals, accompanied by the voice of an unseen narrator.

VOLTS   An electronic measurement of the pressure available at a power source. In North America the standard is 110–120 V.

VOLUME   The measurable loudness of a sound signal.

VOLUME UNIT (VU)   Measurement of audio level. Indicates the average of the sound level, not the peak.

WATTS   Measurement of power used in a piece of electrical or electronic equipment.

WAVEFORM MONITOR An electronic measuring tool; both oscilloscopes and vectorscopes are waveform monitors.

WEDGE Plate fastened to the bottom of a camera that allows it to be quickly mounted to a tripod equipped with a matched slot.

WHITE BALANCE Electronic matching of the camera circuits to the color temperature of the light source.

WHITE LEVEL (Gain) Level of maximum voltage in a video signal.

WILD SOUND Ambient background sound. See **NAT SOUND.**

WIPE Electronic special effects transition that allows one image to be replaced by another with a moving line separating the two pictures. Stopping a wipe in mid-movement creates a split-screen.

WRATTEN A series of filters originally designed for photography but adapted for use in cinematography, videography.

X-AXIS The plane running horizontally to the camera.

XLR PLUG Professional audio connector that allows for three conductors plus a shielded ground. Special types of multi-pin XLRs are used for headsets and battery power connectors.

Y-AXIS The plane running vertically to the camera.

Z-AXIS The plane running away/toward the camera.

ZOOM See **variable focal length lens.**

Index

194